Maida

EMBRACING THE MO...

Ventures with God in Indonesia

What Christian and Missionary Alliance Leaders are saying:

"My path intersected with the Chapmans before they went to Indonesia, when Gordon dedicated our third child while on Mission's tour, then during our two different visits to Indonesia and finally in their retirement years back in Canada. Reports of their adventures in Indonesia and the testimonies of colleagues and alumni confirm the main focus of their work in teaching and the translation of vital materials for the National Church. Surviving Typhoon Hester on their first trip to Indonesia and facing the potential dangers of the 1965 coup d'etat reveal God's faithfulness to two special servants."

—Dr. Melvin Sylvester,
Chancellor of Canadian Bible College and Canadian Theological Seminary

"Gordon and Adina Chapman were just one cohort ahead of me in ministry. During my tenure as Director of Missions and Personnel of the C&MA Canada (1981-1992) they were sprinting down the homeward stretch, engaged in the arduous task of national leadership training. While speaking at the Indonesian National Church Conference in 2001, numbers of national pastors asked me about the Chapmans. Gordon and Adina knew well how to invest in eternity by teaching the future generation of leaders."

—Dr. Arnold Cook,
President of the Alliance World Fellowship

"My wife and I ministered with Gordon and Adina Chapman in Indonesia. We learned valuable lessons from them as they mentored us during our first term. Few missionaries have ever worked harder or served with more passion than the Chapmans. Many Christian workers serving throughout the Indonesian archipelago today are ministering more effectively because of the training they received from Gordon and Adina."

—Dr. Peter Nanfelt,
President of the Christian and Missionary Alliance, USA

"The apostolic pilgrimage of Adina and Gordon Chapman will easily translate into a revived understanding of the struggles and triumphs of those who are called to participate in the great Kingdom Cause! To be a friend of Adina through her missions driven life one soon realizes that Missions is not on the agenda but it *is* the agenda of the church. We highly recommend her and her reminiscences in *Embracing the Mountain*."

—Rev. Gordon Fowler,
Canadian Alliance, Pastoral Care Coordinator

"Gordon and Adina Chapman's ministry had a strategic place in the history of Jaffray Theological College. It still fortifies the work of all their alumni who are leaders in the C&MA national churches and leaders of other church organizations. The quality of their printed lectures, seminars and devotional messages will continue to bear fruit for years to come. Adina's published New Testament Survey text is required reading in our C&MA National Church Bible schools and colleges and in most other theological colleges in Indonesia. As for Gordon, he was always my most valued advisor."

—Dr. Peter Anggu,
President of Jaffray Theological College, Indonesia

EMBRACING THE MOUNTAIN

Ventures with God in Indonesia

by Adina Chapman

Garnet Data

Printed and bound in Canada by Art Bookbindery
Cover design by Darlene Schacht/Art Design

Published in Canada by Garnet Data.
Inquiries: Garnet.Data@MTS.net

National Library of Canada Cataloguing in
Publication

Chapman, Adina
    Embracing the mountain : ventures with
God in Indonesia / by Adina Chapman.

ISBN 0-9734209-0-1

    1. Chapman, Gordon V., 1926-1993.
2. Chapman, Adina.
3. Missionaries--Indonesia--Biography.
 4. Missionaries--Canada--Biography.
5. Christian and Missionary Alliance--Missions-
-Indonesia. I. Title.

BV3342.C42A3 2003   266'.99
               C2003-906547-2

Errata

The author regrets to report an error occurring
on page 134, lines 4-5. Please delete the following sentence:

"During most of our time in Torajaland, we also taught at
Jaffray Theological College in Makassar."

This book is lovingly dedicated to my husband, Gordon,
faithful companion in ministry for forty-six years;
to my children, Kenneth, Richard,
Kathleen, Timothy, Sylvia and their families;
to all of our Indonesian and missionary colleagues in ministry
and to our alumni serving throughout the Indonesian
archipelago—
many of whom play a vital role in this story.

ACKNOWLEDGMENTS

I would like to express my sincere thanks to all the people who made the writing of *Embracing the Mountain* possible:

To my husband, Gordon, whose copious records of annual missionary reports along with so much additional information had no doubt been saved for a permanent record such as this.

To my children who often added their insightful comments and valuable information to make this a more comprehensive and engaging story.

To Indonesian and missionary colleagues whose letters and emails added vital details to this historical account.

To the alumni of our Christian and Missionary Alliance schools and colleges in Indonesia who took the time to freely share the experiences of their lives, whose essential participation in ministry is the essence of God's purpose in expanding His Kingdom.

To the friends of the Indonesian Gospel Fellowship whose records in their "50th Anniversary Celebration" brochure, and their *Year 2000 Supreme Mission of KIBAID* magazine provided invaluable information regarding their challenges in ministry.

And to Sylvia and Gil Geske, Marilynne Foster, Tammy Chapman, and Karen Chapman for their invaluable editing and technical assistance in preparing this book.

TABLE OF CONTENTS

** Note: For the English translation of the following preface
please see Appendix II.

Salam Bahagia di Dalam Kristus Yesus

Kasih karunia dan damai sejahtera dari Allah, Bapa kita, dan dari Tuhan Yesus Kristus menyertai kamu. Dalam kasih Kristus saya mengirim salam kepada, teman-teman sejawat dan para alumni di Indonesia, dengan perkataan rasul Paulus dari 2 Korintus 3:2-3, "Kamu adalah surat pujian kami yang tertulis dalam hati kami dan yang dikenal dan yang dapat dibaca oleh semua orang. Karena telah ternyata, bahwa kamu adalah surat Kristus, yang ditulis oleh pelayanan kami, ditulis bukan dengan tinta, tetapi dengan Roh dari Allah yang hidup, bukan pada loh-loh batu, melainkan pada loh-loh daging, yaitu di dalam hati manusia." *

Sama seperti rasul Paulus memuji Allah karena kesetiaan anak-anak Tuhan di Korintus, demikian juga saya mengucap syukur kepada Tuhan bahwa kalian telah menjadi surat Kristus yang dapat dibaca oleh semua orang untuk kemuliaan Allah dalam pelayanan kalian setempat. Selain itu, saya bersyukur kepada Allah karena Ia telah memberikan kesempatan kepada kami untuk melayani kalian dalam suatu persekutuan yang indah, yang menghiburkan saya sampai sekarang. Semoga kasih Yesus Kristus dan kekuatan Roh Allah senantiasa melengkapi kalian untuk kemuliaan Tuhan dalam pelayanan.

Maafkan jikalau peristiwa-peristiwa yang tertulis dalam penerbitan ini tidak meriwayatkan pengalaman-pengalaman kalian semua. Yang telah tertulis ini hanya menjadi contoh-contoh cara kalian berhasil dengan pertolongan Tuhan di masing-masing daerah. Diharapkan agar apa yang telah dilaporkan, akan menyatakan suatu keseimbangan dalam hal-hal kesulitan yang dialami dengan hasil-hasil yang tercapai.

Dalam segala hal ini saya memuji Tuhan karena Dialah yang memberikan kesempatan kepada kita bersama untuk *memeluk gunung* itu, dengan maksud memperluas Kerajaan Allah bagi kemuliaanNya. "Akan hal ini aku yakin sepenuhnya, yaitu Ia, yang memulai pekerjaan yang baik di antara kamu, akan meneruskannya sampai pada akhirnya pada hari Kristus Yesus." Filipi 1:6 *

Kasih karunia Tuhan Jesus,
Ibu Adina Chapman
—bulan Nopember, tahun 2003

* Kutipan ayat-ayat dari Perjanjian Baru di atas, diselenggarakan oleh *Lembaga Alkitab Indonesia*, di Jakarta 1975.

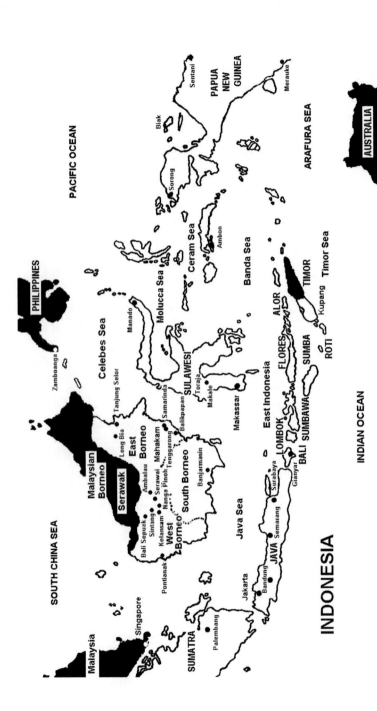

INTRODUCTION

Indonesians have a popular proverb that says: "Maksud hati memeluk gunung. Apa daya? Tangan tak sampai!" (My heart desires to embrace the mountain. What can I do about it? My arms are not long enough!)

We could never do it on our own. However, the building of God's Kingdom in Indonesia would be possible, as together with our Indonesian and missionary colleagues and with the alumni of our schools throughout the Indonesian archipelago, we held hands to "surround the mountain to embrace it". How our Sovereign Commander worked it out in our lives and in theirs would only unfold as time passed. Not only is this a chronicle of our 40 years of service in Indonesia, it is the story of many people whom God brought into our lives. Much of this account is about our friends who have shared stories of how God is extending His Kingdom to this day.

Fundamental to how God prepared each of us to be His emissaries was the way we allowed Him to develop His characteristics in us. Just as the maximum fragrance of a rose is emitted when its petals are pressed, so Christ prepares people for His divine plan. The apostle Paul states the purpose clearly in II Corinthians 2:14, "But thanks be to God, who always leads us in triumphal procession in Christ and through us spreads everywhere the fragrance of the knowledge of him." However, walking in the fragrance of Christ would only be possible if He managed our learning experiences. That was the principle that guided us to gather people who would join us in this triumphal procession.

> *We are here for one purpose only that is to be captives in the train of Christ's triumphs—the absolute captivity of our lives to Jesus Christ. ... Paul's secret joy was to be a captive of the Lord. He had no other interest in heaven or in earth. ... When the Victor has got us so completely, it is His victory ... and we become unto God a sweet fragrance of Christ.*
> —Oswald Chambers, *My Utmost for His Highest*

We observed various responses in our students' submission to the Lord. Sometimes choices were made that led to defeat instead of triumph in Christ. However, the prayers of God's people always played a vital part in restoration. Scripture verifies that God gives people second chances—as in the lives of Abraham, Moses and Jacob in the Old Testament, and Peter and John Mark in the New Testament. It was the Lord who prepared servants for devoted stewardship in ministry. Many of them were taught by Him to persevere in the kind of hard faith that never makes sense outside of a personal relationship with Christ. That was the winning factor.

Together with our Indonesian friends, we also had the example of a revered predecessor who knew the cost of obedience to God. Dr. Robert Jaffray's mission policy was to contact people, to evangelize, to organize and to instruct converts to witness to their countrymen. These were good biblical guidelines as we prepared workers for God's Kingdom, who, in turn would prepare other workers, generation after generation in a perpetual harvest.

The speed with which the Christian faith spread among previously unreached peoples testified to the fact that Dr. Jaffray's vision and goals had divine origin. Gains in one area were consolidated before workers entered new areas, paralleling the New Testament pattern of evangelism. The first Bible school which Robert Jaffray opened in Makassar in 1932 had, by the year 2001, become 28 Christian and Missionary Alliance (C&MA) national church theological schools throughout the Indonesian archipelago, with a total of 3008 students registered that year. They studied at various academic levels, with seven schools at a college level. In the year 2000, teaching sessions to upgrade workers in their abilities were also available. Above all, the goal of theological education has always been to develop leaders for indigenous and self-sustaining movements of church-planting that permeate culture and society.

To add to the formal education process, hundreds of lay people are being trained in various provinces by attending Theological Education by Extension (TEE), a program in which teachers travel from village to village to give lessons to those registered for classes. More recently, colleagues are reaching unreached peoples in community development ministries.

In his keynote address at the 1987 National Workers' Conference, Dr. Peter Anggu, President of Jaffray Theological College (Sekolah Tinggi Theologia Jaffray, or STTJ), stressed the need for the National Church to become a truly missionary organization. That emphasis is so clear in Christ's words in Matthew 9:37b-38, "The harvest is plentiful but the workers are few. Ask the Lord of the harvest, therefore, to send out workers into his harvest field."

The Apostle Paul gives more detailed directives for all true believers in Romans 10:13-15a, "for, 'Everyone who calls on the name of the Lord will be saved.' How, then, can they call on the one they have not believed in? And how can they believe in the one of whom they have not heard? And how can they hear without someone preaching to them? And how can they preach unless they are sent?"

Paul describes how the onus of responsibility includes the whole community of Christians, who are instructed to pray for the Lord of the harvest to send forth labourers who will teach the Word, helping people to believe and be saved so that they can enjoy the Christian life. The church's total responsibility involves more than just sending out workers. Praying for them, encouraging them, and supporting them financially are critical elements of Christ's mandate. May God continue to build His Kingdom in Indonesia through faithful Christians.

Gordon Chapman and Adina Schmidt in Victoria, B.C. in 1945

CHAPTER 1

THE KINGDOM MANDATE

The disciples' decision to obey Jesus after the Ascension proved a pivot point of history. The world was never the same again. The disciples' realization that Christ is who he says he is, compelled them to obedience. This is the historic reality of Christianity.
— Chuck Colson, *Loving God*

Why did we leave the relative comforts of Canada behind in 1952 to go to Indonesian West Borneo (Kalimantan Barat)? Weren't we risking our lives and the lives of our children in this process? Were we ready to face the austerities of hardship and loneliness? Would living among a people with foreign social mores for 40 years be too much of a challenge?

Missionaries whom we met, who had already survived many difficulties, were pleading for committed Christians to join them. It was the same challenge that the Apostle Paul had received from Jesus in Acts 26:17-18, "I am sending you to open their eyes and turn them from darkness to light, and from the power of Satan to God, so that they may receive forgiveness of sins and a place among those who are sanctified by faith in me." To embrace that challenge we had to acknowledge that Jesus, the King of all the earth, would guide us one step at a time.

* * * * * *

John Wesley, English clergyman and founder of Methodism, and his brother Charles, clergyman and hymn writer, had a far-reaching effect on Christianity during the 18th century in the British Isles and beyond. Such was the religious heritage of Gordon's paternal grandparents, and the Lennies, his maternal grandparents. His grandfather, Robert Lennie (1834-1914) became a well-known pastor in his native Scotland, then in England, and later in Canada, traveling as well in some parts of the western United States.

As a young Baptist pastor, Robert Lennie diligently studied the Scriptures, even doing intensive studies on certain doctrines, such as the policy of believers' baptism which his early childhood church fathers had not accepted. Later he realized his ambition to study at Spurgeon's College in London, financing his studies by taking time-consuming, weekend ministries.

Gordon inherited his grandfather's studious and insightful nature. He received Christ in his mid-teens while having dinner with his brother Chuck Chapman and his wife Eily. They themselves had recently become Christians through the messages of *The Lutheran Hour* and Percy Crawford's *Young Peoples Church of the Air*. Subsequently, these Christian radio messages also brought Gordon to faith in Christ as Saviour on January 11, 1942.

While his mother deteriorated in health because of cancer, she received clear, spiritual guidance and comfort from Rev. Fred Landis, pastor of the Victoria Alliance Tabernacle. Because she wanted Gordon to have the same direction for his future, she requested that he be allowed to go to Sunday school and worship services with Chuck and Eily at the Alliance Church. In his early days he had attended another church with his parents.

Gordon's last picture with his mother, taken not long before her death

Gordon's mother greatly inspired him. For example, the humour in the editorial section of the Victoria Daily Colonist always made her laugh hilariously. It was this inherited humour that would see Gordon through many difficult days in the jungles of West Borneo. Throughout his teaching career his students felt doubly blessed by the humour he added to his classes.

In mid-1942 Gordon faced the biggest crisis of his early life. He had the ambition to some day have a home in Victoria with a loving family around him. Yet in his heart there was a hidden call to become a missionary. He thought he could avoid that by becoming an active Christian too late in life to qualify for missionary work. In those days, the Christian & Missionary Alliance (C&MA) had a policy that limited people from becoming missionaries if they were older than 30 years of age. But while his mother lay dying in the hospital he visualized losing her supportive discernment. In his intense anxiety he surrendered his future into God's hands, a major turning point in his life.

What primarily prepared Gordon for his future was his insatiable desire to read. Even in his elementary school days he would arrive early at school and sit on the school steps with a book in hand till the bell rang. Later, reading science fiction expanded his inquisitive mind. Working in the Victoria Public Library during his high school days added much to his general knowledge. Years later, at Jaffray Theological College in Makassar, he would be assigned to be an advisor to the library staff, where he would have the opportunity to recommend the purchase of quality books and cataloguing materials.

During his high school days his spiritual growth was strengthened by attending a weekly Bible study in his brother Chuck Chapman's home. Together with other keen Christian young people, he was nurtured in his faith. Lengthy discussions with his friend, John Richards, broadened his interests in theology. Eventually both of them became Bible school teachers.

His grandfather Robert Lennie's pastoral experiences were often on Gordon's mind during his days in Regina, Saskatchewan, at Western Canadian Bible Institute (later called Canadian Bible College). He especially enjoyed Rev. Downey's theology classes where freedom to participate in discussions challenged his thinking. He spent many hours beyond class requirements studying potential pros and cons of a certain doctrinal issue, until he formulated what to him seemed the only point of truth. He later had the opportunity, in an exam, to use those research findings, filling a legal-sized sheet of paper with his answer. To Gordon's great delight, Rev. Downey gave him full marks for the answer, even predicting that some day he would be a teacher of theology.

Compelling convictions for his future came to Gordon when he heard Rev. Arthur Mouw speak of the Dyaks who embraced Christianity in a mass movement in West Borneo. They had been delivered from the bondage of worshipping evil spirits when they burned their fetishes and began to worship the living God. Rev. Mouw gave Gordon a booklet relating these miraculous deliverances, which became a continuing reminder to him.

Arthur Mouw told of a Dyak man who'd had a dream of three men coming to teach them, a white man and two dark-skinned men. So when Rev. Mouw arrived with two Indonesian workers, the Dyak and his friends were overjoyed and ready to hear about Jesus who could deliver them from the bondage of evil-spirit worship. This miraculous experience opened the doors to their mass movement to Christianity. In a few years other missionaries joined him to reach many more people in remote, upstream areas. The call to develop a strong church among these people compelled Gordon to commit his life to missions. During 1955 to 1967 he taught the following generation of Dyak Christians to become pastors, evangelists and teachers to their people in this area.

To this day church planting and church growth have expanded in an amazing way. In 1967 there was only one theological training school in West Borneo. Today, there are two schools at lower academic levels upcountry, and a college level school in the port city of Pontianak. The students of the 1950s and 1960s continue to reach their own people as the Holy Spirit anoints and blesses them.

Gordon was also deeply influenced with a story related by Rev. Walter Post, a missionary in East Borneo. A native Christian took Rev. Post to a gravesite where his dear mother had been buried. He asked, "My mother died before you came with the messages of Jesus. Will she be in heaven?" What could Walter Post say? There was only one answer. She never had a chance to make a choice. Christians of her generation had been responsible to get the salvation message to her. Likewise, unreached peoples of our generation are our responsibility. Gordon frequently shared this fundamental truth with Christians, especially with his students in Indonesia. It generated a passion to spread the Kingdom message of deliverance in Christ.

The most compelling voice for The Great Commission mandate came when Gordon heard of Dr. Robert Jaffray's experiences. After Dr. Jaffray had been a missionary in China for 35 years, he felt the divine call to begin work in French Indochina (now called Vietnam). Simultaneously, he fulfilled his duties as chairman in Wuchow, China and spearheaded the advance into Vietnam. Under his direction many missionaries arrived to participate in the growing Vietnamese ministry.

The story of Dr. Jaffray's compassion for a lost world, as described by Arthur Mouw, took on a new meaning as he told of his new target for Alliance missions in The Dutch East Indies (now called Indonesia). Ever the trailblazer for missionary work in the Far East, Dr. Jaffray had spent several months in early 1928 sailing throughout parts of the Indonesian archipelago. Names like Samarinda and Balikpapan in East Borneo, Makassar and Pare Pare in Celebes (Sulawesi), Surabaya in Java, and cities in Bali kept echoing in his mind. There were so many signs of people worshipping multiple gods. His heart ached because of the lack of a Christian witness. Dr Jaffray shared his burden with the Board of Managers of the C&MA in New York.

How would they respond? It was just before the 1929 Wall Street Crash. Finances were not readily available. In fact, some mission organizations were obliged to retrench. Dr. Jaffray understood the problem. He'd done what he could. He would return to his work in China. But God had other plans for him.

One night as Dr. Jaffray lay sleeping, he had a dream so vivid and so terrible he could not doubt its meaning. He was fleeing as a fugitive from justice with stains of human blood on his hands. He thought Jesus was pursuing him. Running through a field of newly fallen snow, he scooped up a handful, trying to wash his hands. He awoke and cried out, "Oh Lord Jesus, what does this mean? I have no bloodstains on my hands. I am washed clean in your precious blood."

At once Scripture verses came to mind from Ezekiel 33:7-8, "Son of man, I have made you a watchman for the house of Israel; so hear the word I speak and give them warning from me. When I say to the wicked, 'O wicked man, you will surely die,' and you do not speak out to dissuade him from his ways, that wicked man will die for his sin, and I will hold you accountable for his blood." The Lord used that dream to confirm Dr. Jaffray's desire to extend his missionary work to Indonesia.

By July 1928, only four months after his trip to Indonesia, he had Leland Wang, a Chinese missionary, working in Makassar. A year later, he left China for Indonesia with two more Christian workers, Mr. Lam and Mr. Lin, making Makassar his headquarters. Dr. Jaffray funded this new endeavor himself, with the help of some friends in North America. Within two years of the start of this new mission, which had by then spread into Borneo, five foreign missionaries arrived to join in the task.

In 1945, Dr. Jaffray died of dysentery, at the age of 72, in a Japanese concentration camp in the mountains of South Sulawesi, just two weeks before the end of World War II. His Indonesian brethren could never forget his example of obedience to God. Christians from the Indonesian C&MA organization revered Dr. Jaffray for his sacrificial ministry among them.

This convincing story of the lostness of men without God confirmed Gordon's own call to be a missionary. He would use it often in teaching and preaching in Indonesia.

* * * * * * *

The beginning of my own awareness of the Great Commission came earlier than it had in Gordon's life. I will always remember a vivid experience of my childhood. I awoke one night, feeling an overwhelming sense of God's presence. In Sunday school I had heard the story of God calling the young boy, Samuel, son of Hannah as recorded in I Samuel 1:21-28. Recalling the story, I cried. What was God expecting me to do? Would I be willing to follow Him on an unknown journey? My crying awoke my parents who prayed with me to help me make my commitment to God. I was not yet ten years old.

My first exposure to missionary work came when the Henry Bartel family arrived from China. With other extended family members and friends, they were our guests for an all-day visit at my childhood home in Saskatchewan. The stories the Bartels shared and the memorabilia they showed us made a lasting impression on my young mind.

After the Bartels' visit in our home, I gradually became aware of the Great Commission mandate of Matthew 28:19-20b, "Therefore go and make disciples of all nations, baptizing them in the name of the Father and of the Son and of the Holy Spirit, and teaching them to obey everything I have commanded you." In my late teens at Saskatoon Bible College, missions carried a major emphasis. Reading biographies of Jonathan Goforth of China, Adoniram Judson of Burma, Dr. Albert Schweitzer of Africa and Amy Carmichael's courageous rescue of children in India prepared me for future missionary work.

The risks of missionary service that most tested my commitment came from the story of John and Betty Stam, who worked with Hudson Taylor of the China Inland Mission. Though they were mercilessly beheaded, their wee baby daughter was found by Chinese friends and nourished until she could be returned to her family in North America. That seemed like such a miraculous provision of a loving God. Stories of missionaries that had been murdered during the Boxer Rebellion in China were another test of my commitment. Was I ready for this?

The spiritual heritage from my forefathers was the beginning of my understanding of Christianity. For many generations my ancestors had been influenced by the founder of the Anabaptist movement. In the 16th century in the Netherlands, a Roman Catholic priest named Menno Simons was not comfortable with the religious demands of his organization. He became convinced that the Bible is the highest authority for a man's personal faith and his Christian life. He could no longer teach the doctrines of the Catholic Church. That decision brought much persecution to the followers of Menno Simons' teaching. But the movement went underground and flourished. His followers, called the Mennonites, fled to other countries where they experienced more religious freedom. In the 18th and 19th centuries many of them, including my paternal and maternal ancestors, came to North America from Europe.

It was this strength of faith that kept my parents, Jacob B. and Margaret (Reimer) Schmidt focused in their Christianity. It permeated every area of their lives. Even in the busiest seasons of the year, daily family devotions were never neglected. I remember so well how my father expressed dependence on God to provide for us, for the success of our crops and for the care of our livestock.

On strenuous summer days on the farm, Dad made sure that we'd stop work on time to attend special evangelistic services or camp meetings scheduled by our church. It was on such an occasion that I became a Christian in my childhood. The following morning I had a miraculous experience of joy because Jesus had forgiven me. I was amazed at the beauty of God's creation enhanced with more splendour than I could ever

7

remember it. Though I was too young to understand Christian growth, it wasn't too difficult to seek forgiveness and keep in touch with my dear Saviour.

During my infancy, the most far-reaching news event was the signing of the Armistice Agreement between the warring factions at the end of World War I, on November 11, 1918. But much more critical to my family's survival was the sweeping effect of the Asian flu epidemic. Before I turned one year old, my mother, then terminally ill with cancer, became a flu victim. For my father, with five children aged one to 11 years, the death of his cherished wife became almost unbearable. How he survived that crisis along with the maintenance of the farm depended in large part on his faith in God's love and care of his family. He married a young widow who helped him through those painful days.

Another devastating event that shaped our Christian strength was the influence of the Great Depression in the early 1930s. We were forced to devise methods of survival. In some ways we had a better chance of maintaining a livelihood than city folks. My life on the farm compared to Gordon's growing-up years in the city was so different. But in our early years as missionaries in Borneo, both country and city lifestyle experiences taught essential lessons that sustained our survival and ministry.

My father's concern for unchurched neighbours in our community also affected me. He arranged for meetings in a nearby schoolhouse, inviting an evangelist as special speaker. During my impressionable teens, his great Christian example gave me an easy transition to traveling in gospel team ministries around the country. During my training days in Saskatoon Bible College we were assigned to teach children in isolated communities in the summer. It was the beginning of personally sharing the love of Jesus with both children and adults.

Pastors and missionaries with their families who were frequent guests in our home also made a lasting impression on my life. When my parents became charter members of the First Alliance Church in Saskatoon, Saskatchewan, the C&MA's mission emphasis strengthened my faith and commitment.

Feeling ill-equipped for missionary work, I decided to train as a registered nurse at the Royal Jubilee Hospital in Victoria, B.C. where my academic qualifications were accepted. There, at the Alliance Church, I met the Chapman family and enjoyed the enthusiastic young people's group. Gordon's brother, Chuck, and his dear wife, Eily, warmly received the Christian nurses into their home. When Gordon's and my mutual priority in missions became obvious, it brought our lives into focus for God's plans. We were married in 1947.

Together we started preparing for a missionary career. We had eight months of missionary experience at Dr. McClean's Nootka Mission Hospital at Esperanza, on the west coast of Vancouver Island. That was basic "boot-camp" training! As staff members of the hospital we went on trips to minister in mining, lumber and fish-cannery towns. We maneuvered the Shantymen's mission boats up and down the channels, often in very hostile weather conditions, one of many new experiences. The west coast of Vancouver Island is called "the graveyard of the Pacific". It was frightening to navigate the narrow channels in the inky darkness of night while sharp rocks jutted out of the water and

Adina Schmidt, graduate of
Royal Jubilee Hospital in Victoria, B.C.

steep cliffs constantly stood nearby. Only God could safely guide us home. Years later we faced similar navigation problems in West Borneo, where mission boats were our only choice of travel to go any distance.

After boot camp, we did two years of home service at Capital Hill Alliance Church in Burnaby, B.C., which provided special training in developing Christian ministry. We also received short interim training at the Seven Oaks Alliance Church and the Revelstoke Alliance Church in B.C. We found these assignments to be valuable internship opportunities.

At the Summer Institute of Linguistics (SIL), held at the University of Oklahoma, we learned to work cross-culturally with an unreached people-group. The SIL's main focus of teaching linguistic principles was especially advantageous to Gordon when he later translated essential materials for students in theological schools throughout the Indonesian archipelago. It was reassuring to know that our God, who knew the end from the beginning, had set many plans in place for the right time.

Gordon and Adina Chapman with sons, Ken (centre) and Richard (seated) taken just prior to their embarking for Indonesia in 1952

CHAPTER 2

<u>SURVIVING TYPHOON HESTER</u>

Others went out on the sea in ships; they were merchants on the mighty waters. They saw the works of the Lord ... For he spoke and stirred up a tempest that lifted high the waves. They mounted up to the heavens and went down to the depths; in their peril their courage melted away. ... Then they cried out to the Lord in their trouble, and he brought them out of their distress. He stilled the storm to a whisper; the waves of the sea were hushed. They were glad when it grew calm, and he guided them to their desired haven.
—Psalm 107:23-26, 28-30

* * * * * * *

By February 1952 we were ready to embark for Indonesia, but our visas hadn't arrived. Were they lost? It became a long wait! All but forgotten, the files finally surfaced at the Makassar Police Office. Eventually, in November we were on our way by train from Vancouver, B.C. to Oakland, California for the first lap of our journey.

For many years The Home of Peace in Oakland was a transition facility for missionaries departing for their field assignments. Kind staff helped us with last minute buying, packing, crating and shipping of our goods. They also provided transportation. They were a wonderful support system for those of us who faced the unknown.

On December 17, 1952, we boarded the *S.S. Steel Artisan* of the Isthmian Steamship Company at the Oakland Naval Base. This freighter was heavily loaded with military equipment destined for Subic Bay, the U.S. Naval Base near Manila, and then for Saigon, French Indochina (Vietnam). The passengers were Mrs. Hewitt, who was traveling to Singapore to visit family; Ralph and Elva Romine with their small child, heading for Grace Christian High School in Manila; Gordon and I with our two little boys, Kenny and Richy, who were on our way to Indonesia; and Mr. Kasiman from Indonesia, who had studied in the United States. Because Mr. Kasiman had overstayed his time, he was being deported. At every port police boarded to guard him. He was actually a gentle fellow.

For about ten days we sailed peacefully, a most enjoyable journey. Throughout the trip we were sumptuously fed. We spent our days watching the bow of our freighter cut through smooth, green waters. Little flying fish darted about just above the surface of the sea. We were surprised to discover that while sitting in the shade on the deck, merely the sun's reflection on the water's surface badly burned us. On Christmas day we crossed the International Date Line and enjoyed a few more peaceful days. The quiet did not last.

Suddenly a strange phenomenon appeared. The rather peaceful ocean's surface actually began to fizz like soda water because of the drastic change in the barometric pressure. The air pressure above the water was so low that air from the sea was escaping into the atmosphere. Our ship's crew recognized the warning signs. The Artisan's radio operator

S.S. Steel Artisan, December 1952

received word that Typhoon Hester was approaching from the south. Such typhoons, with hurricane-force winds, were common in the western Pacific Ocean and the South China Sea at that time of year.

The crew checked over the life boats and tested all the steel cables that fastened the heavy war equipment to the decks. Above the military apparatus, heavy-duty catwalks were also tested for their durability. It was eerie! The crew tried to assure us that they were performing a routine check. Actually, it was much more.

Frightening news reported 50-foot waves pounding the shores of Guam. Our Captain wanted to avoid entering the Philippine Islands at the time the typhoon was scheduled to arrive there. We would certainly be dashed against the rocks in the force of the ferocious winds. Hoping to steer clear of the storm altogether, he ordered our freighter to veer north to get out of harm's way. To maintain a slight headway in the fierce gale, he ordered the ship's engines slowed to a minimum—just enough to control the ship's direction. He hoped to enter the islands after the typhoon passed.

Our radio operator received word that winds near the center of Typhoon Hester had reached 200 miles per hour. Around us the gale's velocity steadily increased. Gordon stood in the open doorway on the lee side of the ship marveling at the force of the angry waves. He watched as the ship approached a 40-foot hole in the sea and was forcefully pitched into it. As the rudder became exposed to the air, the freighter shuddered violently, struggling to maintain its course. Time and time again the great vessel shook uncontrollably.

A 50-foot wave hit the starboard side of the ship and washed over the bridge, spilling sea water down the stairs to the decks below. One mate, phoning the engine room from the bridge, fell when he had nothing to hang on to. The fire extinguisher beside him was knocked off its moorings, spewing its slippery contents over everything. The mate rolled back and forth across the deck together with the extinguisher, making it very difficult for him to get back on his feet. He was the only person who sustained any major injuries throughout the whole storm. He had a wrenched thumb, a wrenched shoulder, bruised ribs and a 3-inch gash above his left eye. As soon as possible, Nurse Elva Romine and I used the ship's first-aid equipment to suture the gash above his eye. When we arrived at the U.S. Naval Base, the mate reported in at their medical facility. They commented that the wound had been repaired in fine form, thanks to Elva who had been an emergency room nurse.

Surrounded by winds that raged ever more furiously, Ralph and Elva Romine joined us in our cabin to pray. Reading Mark 4:35-41 seemed very relevant. Jesus had stilled that fearful storm for the disciples. We asked Him to do the same for us. We were comforted by the words of Psalm 91, which promised that the Lord would command His angels to guard us in all our ways and deliver us in our troubles. We also claimed God's promises as we read Acts 27:21-44 where, in part, Paul said to the 275 people on board, "I urge you to keep up your courage, because not one of you will be lost; … Not one of you will lose a single hair from his head … everyone reached land in safety." It encouraged us to trust God to guide us into port unharmed.

Damages to the ship and its contents were staggering. By the night of January third, the ship's rolling became very critical as again and again giant waves smashed into *The Steel Artisan*. Gordon and I lay on the outer edges of the toddlers' bunks to support them against the wall. It was comfort enough to get them back to sleep. On that fearful night I sang and prayed nonstop during the worst of the storm. The Psalmist said, "You kept my eyes from closing; I was too troubled to speak … I remembered my songs in the night." (Psalm 77:4, 6) By dawn the freighter was listing more than 15 degrees. Though the crew tried to stabilize the ship it was a futile effort. Once the storm passed we slept with our mattresses on the deck. It was the only way we could get to sleep without falling out of bed.

During the severest gale force winds, we heard frightening "ping" noises as the one-inch steel cables snapped. They had been used to secure the 12-ton tanks of tar and other heavy cargo in place on the main deck. Eleven tanks of tar from the starboard side, which were to be used for runways and asphalt roads in Subic Bay, washed overboard. A 16-ton truck and various other pieces of military equipment were also lost. A heavy winch and some loading booms lay on the deck, knocked off of their moorings. The storm badly bent the ship's largest boom.

During the storm, drums of tar in the ship's cargo space were knocked out of their crates and rolled back and forth in the hold of the ship. Crew members rushed in to stop the mayhem. The small crates they grabbed to push under the sides of the drums were immediately crushed under the weight of the big tanks. Suddenly, as fumes of household ammonia began to fill the hold, the crew abandoned their work and quickly escaped to the fresh air outside. Later, on inspection at Subic Bay, the holds revealed large crates full of badly damaged furniture. What was left of their crating looked like kindling. In some holds the tar from broken tanks had spilled all over the cargo.

One large tank of tar from the upper deck rolled overboard and later washed back onto the deck. As it split open, its contents spilled over a large area. For many weary hours during the heat of the day, the crew tried scooping up the tar with shovels. It was a useless effort. Finally, when they put ice from the ship's refrigeration system on the tar, they were able to chip it away to load into drums.

"Stand by for fire on the after-deck!" was the frightening call that came during the worst of the storm. Tanks of explosive liquefied petroleum gas had been firmly secured in a strong crate on the back deck. As the crating was crushed, the tanks rolled around freely knocking off some of their valves. Gas fumes filled the air, even penetrating the cracks in our portholes. Thank God an explosion never occurred for we would not have survived it. During the worst of the storm it was suicidal for a crewman to venture out on deck. He would surely have been blown into the sea unless he had a rope tied around his waist to keep him tethered to the ship.

As we approached the eye of the typhoon, the wind velocity reached 200 miles per hour. Quite suddenly, we hit the eye of the storm and cruised in calm waters. After almost an hour, just as suddenly as we had entered, we were back in the fierce tempest again. The captain knew that when one is in the eye of the storm, any direction is the quickest way out. After another eight hours we had escaped the worst of the furious winds.

Why did it take three long days to get into the fury of that storm? Instead of ending in the Philippines, it ended in Japan. The radio news from Guam had been misleading. The typhoon had changed course, so we did not avoid it after all. Before it was over, the captain had spent 72 hours on the bridge and 48 hours on his feet as he directed his steersmen to guide the ship. Throughout the storm, the radio operator remained on alert nonstop. His main antenna had stretched ten feet and finally broke. With a shorter emergency antenna he was able to transmit directions regarding the course of the typhoon.

After the hurricane-force winds ceased, both the captain and the radio man emerged from their long, exhausting vigil looking like death warmed over. Their faces portrayed a ghastly pallor. Great, black circles accentuated their sunken eyes. The operator's fingers on his left hand were severely lacerated from gripping the steel desk while operating the radio with his right hand. Weary in every bone and muscle, both men suffered from total fatigue and took an extended time for recovery.

The captain said that in 48 years of sailing this was the worst storm he had ever encountered. When we left Oakland, California, our freighter had been fully loaded. When we arrived at Subic Bay, the starboard side of the deck was swept clean. The ship and

17

its contents suffered incredible damage. Cargo in the holds had shifted dangerously. We listed so badly that when the boat rolled, the freighter's inclinometer recorded the roll beyond 45 degrees. The captain admitted that he feared the ship could not be saved. What I had felt and feared was not my imagination. How miraculous that we had stayed afloat in spite of the imbalance of the cargo! We should not have survived. God protected our ship from capsizing. Our Commander in Chief still had other plans for us.

Lloyds of London, our freighter's insurance company, examined the cargo when we anchored in port. They were incredulous that we had survived. They reported it as one of the worst typhoons in marine history. When our ship sailed into port it listed at a dangerous angle, looking like a rusty wreck that yearned for a major overhaul and a paint job. It was a far cry from the beautiful freighter that left the California Naval Base 20 days earlier. In fact, another freighter, which had not gone through the eye of the storm had broken up, and all on board were drowned.

God, who controls all things, had brought our damaged, listing ship into a safe haven. He had answered our prayers and the prayers of many of our friends. Mrs. E. Hoffman was one who had specifically been directed by the Lord to pray for us. In a letter she wrote:

Dear Mr. & Mrs. Chapman,

It is almost 20 years since we said good bye in the Saskatoon Alliance Church. ... This Sunday your daughter Kathy from the Bible College [Canadian Bible College in Regina, SK] came to visit me. After I found out that she is your daughter, I told her that I know you. ... After you left Saskatoon, one night I had an unusual experience. I woke up, and it was as if somebody said, "Pray for the Chapmans." I was shocked. But then and there I prayed for you, not knowing why, nor what this was about. ... I marked the date on my calendar. ... A month after that I found out that you had big troubles on the sea, and your ship was in danger. Such an experience I have never had before, or since then. I remember you often in my prayers. ... Your daughter was quite excited when I told her my story. Her last words were, "Don't forget to write to my parents." ... I hope God is blessing your work in Indonesia.

E. Hoffmann,
November 7, 1973

* * * * * * *

Prayer does not equip us for the greater work;
prayer is the greater work.

—Oswald Chambers

Boat-building in Kalimantan, Borneo in the 1950s

CHAPTER 3

<u>SCARS OF WAR</u>

In the inner harbor of Manila Bay rusty hulks of partially submerged warships stood like ugly skeletons against the tropical sky, grotesque reminders of the ravages of death from World War II. In the midst of it all emerged the flourishing tropical growth of trees and flowers after refreshing rains. What a contrast of life and death as we stepped ashore in the Philippines. The picture drew a perfect analogy between the state of sinful man destined for judgment, and the new creation of a born-again believer, made alive in Christ by His divine touch of restoration. This inexplicable wonder of the Lord's recreative power—the stamp of His image in our lives—is the most marvelous miracle ever conceived by God. His Word reiterates it so well, "As for you, you were dead in your transgressions and sins, ... But because of his great love for us, God, who is rich in mercy, made us alive with Christ ..." (Ephesians 2:1, 4-5a)

At the waterfront, palm trees waving in the breeze lined Dewey Boulevard like sentinels. We were told that this rather wide, straight boulevard had been used as a runway by the Japanese Air Force during World War II. Bomb-damaged buildings in downtown Manila still remained in ruins eight years after the war had ended, providing shelter for the very poor. Most streets looked squalid and unkempt.

But there was enchantment in the city. Colourful, privately owned *jeepneys* winding their way through the streets, provided ample transportation. Or, if preferred—as we did—we hired a small pony-driven buggy, after striking a bargain, of course. With no roof overhead, we had full view of the street-side markets that displayed an array of fruits and vegetables which we had never seen. Beautiful flowers and a variety of spices wafted their fragrant aromas. However, not all smells were pleasant. Diverse, malodorous scents, which we gradually learned to accept, would also be a part of the market landscape everywhere in the Orient.

It was fascinating to see the beauty of life in the countryside. A Christian friend we met took us for a 60-kilometer ride to see what rural agriculture looked like. Coconut, banana and papaya groves waved gently in the morning breeze. Though some rice paddies were still green, in others the farmers harvested and winnowed rice. The popular oriental water buffalo—their work horses—stood visible everywhere. Driving farther on, we viewed the picturesque scenery of a lake in the middle of a volcanic mountain. Coming out of the hot and humid lowlands, the mountain air refreshingly cooled our skin.

Back in Manila, Ralph and Elva Romine and their little boy, our companions through the typhoon experience, headed for Grace Christian High School. Mr. Spahr, the principal of the school, invited us to join them in a fellowship time where Rev. Raymond Frame of the China Inland Mission shared from the Word of God. The meeting ended in a renewing prayer time. After that, we attended a birthday party at the home of the vice principal of the school. She had prepared a sumptuous Chinese meal, concluding with cake and ice cream.

On our Sunday in Manila we went ashore to join friends at The First Baptist Church. That afternoon we were invited to attend a welcome celebration for the Romines. There, we were introduced to a Chinese Christian gentleman whose brother was a member of parliament in Jakarta, Indonesia. Later, we had a very pleasant visit with the brother in Jakarta. Another man we met in Manila said that this Chinese man had helped our Indonesian C&MA staff with translation work. What a small world!

After the most essential repairs to our damaged freighter were completed, we continued to Saigon, our next stop. For several days we had an uneventful trip. However, on arrival at Port St. Jacques, the mouth of the river that would take us to Saigon, pilots came on board to guide us for the 3-hour trip. We were advised not to go on deck. This area had been declared a war zone. Gun boats, with machine guns mounted on their bows, patrolled the river constantly. Since many of the crew were on the decks, we finally ventured out to get a better view of the countryside.

Fishing boats were tied up against the lush delta. With their colourful sails they looked like flagships lined up along the shore. A dozen cargo vessels—tied together, were being towed upriver by tugboats. They carried rice, rubber and other raw materials. We were told that families often spent their entire lives on these boats.

In the late afternoon our freighter's crew moored the vessel at the river's edge. They would begin to unload the cargo the next morning. Unfortunately, much of the equipment destined for the American Army in Vietnam, had been lost overboard during the typhoon. For them it was a great loss.

An immigration officer came aboard to inquire about passengers. Hearing that we were missionaries, he immediately spoke of "Mission Evangelique", and gave us the address of the C&MA guest house. As we looked over the rail, who should we see but John Sawin, the Alliance business agent for Vietnam. He came aboard and invited us to dinner. He informed us that they had been waiting for our arrival for the past several days. However, the first mate didn't want us to go ashore on the shaky wooden ladder suspended from the side of the ship. It was the only exit available to us. After a long wait no gangplank arrived. There was nothing else to do but use that shaky ladder.

We enjoyed a delightful dinner and a visit with all the missionaries at the guest house. In the late afternoon we returned to the ship. The next morning we again went ashore to see some of the city. Streets lined with the usual tropical vegetation looked orderly and clean. We hired a cyclo-pedicab for a pleasant ride back to the guest house.

The following day we had a memorable visit in the home of senior missionaries, Irving and Mary Stebbins. Rev. Stebbins took us to see their newest church building. It was encouraging to know that this congregation was building their own worship place and was already self-supporting. Mission finances merely helped with some of the building costs. It was a great example of what we anticipated in our future.

In 1974, twenty-two years later, all the missionaries and thousands of nationals fled Vietnam, as the Viet Cong took over the country. Many who fled in rickety boats never survived. But by the late 1990s, in spite of severe suffering under Viet Cong rule, history recorded that the church in Vietnam had grown by leaps and bounds. God has literally brought life out of death.

Next we sailed for Bangkok, but we actually dropped anchor in the Gulf of Siam, beyond sight of the city. Unfortunately, we didn't have visas to go ashore at that time. Years later we would have opportunity to visit Bangkok a few times to see the exotic displays of Thai culture and observe their religious activities. We would watch them in their rituals, bowing at the gold-decked images in their temples as they appealed to their gods for peace and prosperity.

What we saw of Thailand at that time, as cargo was being unloaded, became a vital education. The longshoremen set up simple tents on the stern of our freighter to stay for the duration of the unloading time. The workers quickly transferred their freight to cargo vessels to be taken to Bangkok. Ordinary farmers came alongside the ship in unique outboard motorboats to peddle their wares.

Many of the longshoremen had something like a wad of chewing tobacco in their mouths. Siam had long been known for its trade in opium. We saw some of the men actually using needles for a quick fix. Sometimes they would be fast asleep on the deck in the middle of a working day—probably under the influence of the drug. This habit was obviously a yoke of death in their unhealthy lifestyle. A shoe, a can or even a block of wood seemed adequate for a pillow. Their beds were simple grass mats on the hard deck. Their lives seemed totally void of any creature comforts. Lit joss sticks tied to the rail were evidence of their attempt to get help from their gods. These were our observations from the upper deck of our ship.

We enjoyed Christian radio programs from the Far East Broadcasting Company (FEBC) in Manila during all our sailings in the Orient. They gave us news of happenings in the Far East and provided a variety of programs in English. It was like a voice from home. Later in Borneo, when we had to depend on this vital contact for news affecting our children, who were far away at boarding school, FEBC provided an information lifeline.

Jakarta, the capital city of Indonesia, was to be our last temporary residence. At four o'clock in the morning, as we sailed along the shores of the Malay Peninsula, we passed the lights of Singapore. With that, we also crossed the equator. Soon we saw numerous small lights off the port side, our first sight of the Indonesian Islands. We began packing our bags and steamer trunk in preparation for arrival. We had now been on *The Steel Artisan* for about six weeks.

As we approached the port we saw a few freighters anchored just inside the breakwater. However, *The Steel Artisan* squeezed into its own Isthmian Steamship berth. Once again, the port agent and immigration officials came on board. We each received a card that had to be given to the immigration officer in Makassar within

14 days. It would indeed take that long before we could get a national passenger liner to take us there.

Just before the serving of the noon meal, an agent of the Dutch Missions Consulate came on board to take us ashore. Our field director in Makassar, Sulawesi, had assigned him to look after us while in Jakarta. After a meal together, he prepared us to go through customs. We took only essential baggage for our next two weeks. The rest would be trans-shipped to Makassar. Gordon's Winchester gun had to be checked with the Superior Customs Officer. We would need a permit from the Minister of War to import it. Though Gordon tried for many months to get that permit, he was never successful. God knew we would never need it.

Back at the port of Tandjong Priok, near Jakarta, the customs desk cleared us and checked us through two more controls. Finally, we were on our way to Hotel Benvenuto. We were later told that though "Benvenuto" was a good name—it was not a good hotel. But circumstances had compelled us to stay there. Just off the shores of Jakarta there had been a collision of two Dutch passenger liners. The captains of these two ships usually greeted each other in passing. During their greeting this time, they were suddenly too close for safety, damaging the bows of both ships. While repairs were made, the passengers of these two large liners were booked into almost every available hotel space. What was left for us couldn't even qualify as a one-star hotel. At least the hotel manager spoke English.

What an introduction to Indonesia! Our room was situated on the ground floor and had a verandah with padded rattan chairs. The room rent, including meals, was a dollar a day Canadian per adult. Being on a main street put us in easy access to street venders. The fresh fruit and cans of biscuits they offered were welcome additions to our diet. With an English/Indonesian dictionary in hand, bartering with the peddlers was our first language learning experience.

Dining was rather simple. Western-style food—breads, simple spreads and some cold cuts constituted our breakfasts and evening meals. Tea and coffee and small amounts of fresh fruit were available with our meals. However the substantial noon meal was always served with hot, red-pepper seasonings, a painful experience for our little boys!

A large bed, with limited sheeting, sparsely furnished our hotel room. Above the bed, a frame five feet high held up the mosquito net for protection against night insects. There was one portable clothes closet with doors. An army cot provided simple sleeping space for our two boys. Poles tied vertically to the cot's frame at each end secured the mosquito net. A small writing table and a chair completed the furnishings. Our latticed bedroom window and verandah doors allowed adequate ventilation, but it also provided an entrance for those pesky night-creatures. And every day, in a small corner hand-basin, I washed our family laundry.

Out the door and around to the back of the hotel was a small room. There, a water reservoir about 3-feet-square, with a dipper on its ledge, was available when we wanted to take a bath. The room had a muddy floor dotted by a few rocks and some old tiles to stand on while you took that dipper bath. There was no door on that bathroom. Wearing a sarong was the only privacy available. It was an initiation for many more such experiences in upcountry places in Indonesia.

To our dismay, huge rats invaded our room. They chewed holes in our unwashed clothes until I learned to lock them in the closet for the night. They also chewed the cords that secured the boys' mosquito net. One morning I awoke to see that both the net and the poles had collapsed on the boys. The management just tied the mosquito net up again.

Unfamiliar night noises often kept me awake. People spent the evening on our verandah chairs, talking in muffled tones while enjoying their cigarettes. Who knows, perhaps they kept us safe from thievery. For several nights there were also loud voices and raucous disturbances outside our window. One woman screamed hysterically. I wondered what her painful crisis might be. Perhaps it was better I didn't know. The next day we were told that she had finally been taken away.

The time came for us to leave for Makassar. The Dutch Missions Consulate agent came to help us board the KPM Dutch passenger ship for the last lap of our journey. It was a great relief to greet our mission chairman, Rev. Wesley Brill, along with two missionary colleagues who came to help us through customs and take us to the mission guest house.

I could not stop a few tears as we sat at our first meal with friends. Mrs. Brill thought I was lonely because we were far away from family in Canada. Yes, I thought of them a lot. But at that point, I was simply overwhelmed at God's care over us in all our experiences from the time we had left Victoria almost three months before.

We were housed in an old building, a pre-World War II house on the campus of the Makassar Bible School, later called Jaffray Bible College. The main guest house had actually been Dr. Robert Jaffray's residence. The campus was protected by a high, barbed wire enclosure. We often heard gunfire at night because of rebel activity, an aftermath of World War II. Only convoys could travel the 20-mile stretch to the nearest airport. In the city we didn't walk outside at night unless we were in a group. In spite of these limitations we felt comparatively safe in the enclosed campus.

Language study began immediately. A high school teacher who was assigned to teach us thought it incredible that we should be assigned to begin with simple grade one to grade three primers. Time and time again he asked us to memorize long lists of words without the context of sentence structure. But we kept taking him back to our simple readers. He knew no English, and we knew no Indonesian. After three months we finally were able speak in simple sentences, and language learning progressed more rapidly. With a total of six months of language study, we were able to do our buying in the market, carry on simple conversations in Indonesian and understand a few things in worship services. This was the method of language acquisition at that time. In later years a better program was put into place.

After we could speak in simple sentences, an interesting thing happened. One day in class when I opened with prayer, I thanked the Lord for our salvation in Jesus, and our sure hope of heaven. The teacher objected to what I had said, because in his mind we couldn't be sure of heaven till we died. I assured him that we could know it now, and quoted John 5:24, "I tell you the truth, whoever hears my word and believes him who sent me has eternal life and will not be condemned; he has crossed over from death to life." He thanked me for sharing this wonderful truth. He was actually a choir director in his church.

By late August we were ready to leave for West Borneo and Nanga Ambalau, the most interior government outpost in the province. In Pontianak, the port city of West Borneo, we bought adequate supplies for an initial period to augment our outfit brought from Canada. Missionaries were there to guide us in our purchases and to take us upstream. In addition to food, we also had to purchase drums of fuel to use on our trip and fuel to use at our Ambalau station. We traveled for five days upriver before meeting our first missionary colleagues in Balai Sepuak. After a few days of rest we were on our way again. Several missionary friends accompanied us on the five-week journey. They made the many new experiences in our travels safe and tolerable. We traveled up the Kapuas River, the Melawi River and finally the Ambalau River.

Unfortunately, it was still the dry season. The level of water in the rivers was hardly adequate for good navigation. We had basic eating and sleeping facilities on board the boat, which had a simple roof and a partially closed-in section. Daily, at dusk we tied up along the shoreline, and at the first crack of dawn we started on our way again. After about ten days of travel we encountered dangerous and unnerving turbulent rapids.

We'd had no white-water rafting experience. When we looked straight ahead, the swift current made it appear like we were traveling very fast. But a glance at the shore proved we were hardly moving ahead at all. In fact, because we were going against the current, it sometimes took several tries to progress ever so slightly. We would have a short distance of smooth sailing and then be suddenly faced again with more raging rapids. The test was to avoid dangerous rocks submerged just below the water's surface. For our experienced missionary friends who had navigated the rapids many times before, there were telltale signs in the swirling water indicating places to avoid. But for us as newcomers it was a frightening episode. On one such occasion, little Kenny was terrified and exclaimed, "Let's pray!" So we prayed. Indeed, in our hearts we were constantly praying most earnestly for God's protection.

When we arrived at Nanga Ambalau, emotional release was more than palpable. It was not the end of the world, but you could see it from there. That's what it felt like when we arrived. As we left our insecure vessel and hit *terra firma* my heart sang praises to our Divine Protector. We had finally reached our place of ministry! Now the real purpose of our coming could begin to unfold. Would our years of training and preparation be sufficient? In fact, we would be tested again and again. We would have to trust our God for the uncharted challenges ahead. One dear old saint by the name of Overton penned:

> *There's so much now I cannot see,*
> *My eyesight's far too dim,*
> *But come what may, I'll simply trust,*
> *And leave it all to Him.*

Adina Chapman administering penicillin during Clinic Day
in Balai Sepuak, Borneo

CHAPTER 4

<u>JUNGLE NURSING ADVENTURES</u>

A nurse is coming! That was the message the village people heard long before my arrival. Person-to-person news travels fast in the remote jungle. Was I qualified to face the daunting confrontations of jungle medical work? I took Registered Nurses' training as it was available in the mid-1940s. I'd had a one-year's obstetrics internship at a small midwifery establishment with hands-on experience. I also had an obstetrics manual, several other basic medical books, a limited number of instruments and a letter from the Provincial Health Office in Pontianak, West Borneo, which contained a permit to practice health care. I also received regular printouts from the Missionary Medical Association that were useful for people in my position, describing treatments for various tropical diseases. Above all, I would have to exercise fervent faith in God to help me with the unknowns.

Whatever credentials I had were farthest from my mind when the urgency of one man's need required immediate attention. He came early one morning after having tangled with a swordfish. The sharp point of the bony sword structure was embedded in the fleshy part of the palm of his hand just below the fingers. It had penetrated the small finger side. His friends had chopped off the protruding portion and brought him to me.

At the time, the shipment of my medical supplies hadn't yet arrived. The only solution I could see was to do what I saw my farmer-father do. A cow had broken through a barbed wire fence and had torn a big gash in her teat. Father tied her down in a lying position. Then using an ordinary sewing needle and white thread he repaired it. Without my medical instruments, I would have to try a similar procedure. I thoroughly cleansed the man's hand. In lieu of a needle driver, I simply sterilized a pair of pliers. With them I sterilized some white thread, a sewing needle and a sharp razor blade.

Fortunately, the bone of the swordfish was embedded near the skin. Therefore I wouldn't encounter major veins or arteries. If I merely pulled the bone out, its sharp opposing barbs would tear deep, bleeding grooves in his flesh. Instead, with a new razor blade, I cut the man's skin right over the embedded fish bone, and lifted the offending object out. At that moment a missionary colleague behind me fainted, falling to the floor. Since I was obviously preoccupied, her husband had to attend to her.

I sprinkled an antibiotic of sulfa crystals on the wound. Then using the pair of pliers and the threaded needle, I carefully sutured up the epidermal skin to completely cover the subcutaneous layers. With that covering the wound would heal faster. I cleansed it, applied clean dressings and asked him to keep it dry for at least a week. The man was so proud of his quick recovery that it made me an instant miracle-woman in the community.

People frequently came asking for pills to treat fevers that displayed malarial symptoms. Quinine pills, produced from the bark of the Indonesian cinchona tree, were available in most towns throughout the country. I always kept a supply on hand. Other villagers came with tropical sores looking like yaws, which I could treat with penicillin injections. People soon thought the miracle injection was a cure for everything. However, I only gave injections as needed.

Intestinal parasites were another common problem. I had several kinds of worm medicine I could give a patient depending on their symptoms. Information I received from the Missionary Medical Association was very helpful in determining which medication to use.

A young man walking through the jungle was carrying a load on his shoulders. Hearing a noise overhead, he looked up and was suddenly hit on one side of his face with a falling durian. Durian is a heavy fruit about the size of a soccer ball with large, thorny spikes. The thorns pierced his skin and some had actually punctured his eyeball. I could pull the thorns out of his skin but could do nothing with the pierced eyeball. Unfortunately he lost his vision in that eye and became very depressed. What village girl would marry a one-eyed man? The emotional damage took longer to heal than his physical injury.

A village woman had been impaled by a long bamboo arrow that was set as a trap to catch a wild boar or a small deer. She had not seen the sign that villagers place on the path near the prepared trap. As she tripped the cord attached to the dangerous weapon, the arrow ripped through one leg in the middle of her thigh and also hit her second thigh. Her husband pulled the arrow out, carried her to his canoe and brought her to me. With a small catheter I flushed the puncture wounds with a cleansing solution every day, and I gave her some antibiotic pills. She was sure she would never walk again, but she did.

A monkey bit a teenage boy. It was not a deep wound. So with a simple cleansing, a suturing procedure and some medication, he was on his way to recovery. By the way, that monkey had been caught for food for the family. We even got a taste of that monkey meat!

A motherless infant was brought to me in a pitiful condition. The father and grandmother had done their best to keep it alive. But they had no sense of the importance of cleaning feeding bottles and nipples. Apparently a wet nanny was not available. Constant diarrhea, a very sore mouth and no doubt a similar intestinal infection gave little hope for the baby's survival. I gave them a special healing powder to dissolve and use in lieu of whatever they used to bottle feed her. I had no clinic facility to give the baby many weeks of constant care and the family didn't have the wisdom to manage the baby's recovery. I despaired of giving any useful assistance. I don't know if the child lived since I didn't hear from them again.

Another infant was brought to me who had fallen the distance of several feet—from the doorway of a house on stilts—onto rocks on the ground. It had an injured neck and was crying in constant pain. I fixed a soft bark fracture frame and securely tied it into this form. I instructed the parents not to take it out of its protective shell. When I gave the baby a mild sedative it went to sleep. About a week later the parents were back. The baby was now having frequent convulsions. They had taken it out of its fracture frame to bathe it in the river. I couldn't believe that they'd taken the baby out of the frame. In their minds, no infant could survive without daily bathing in the river. The baby had sustained fatal injuries. Large, bruised areas were visible on its neck. How could they possibly manage that injury in their lifestyle?

These two cases troubled me deeply. I could not set up a routine clinic system for we would be away from our Ambalau home for months at a time, and in the end we lived up there for only about one-and-a-half years. Families who came with their sick provided their own lodging. I merely gave them medication and simple treatments. That was the common practice for our outpatient services in the province.

People generally chewed at lot of sirih, or betelnut. They claimed it gave them stamina and relieved pain. In reality, a harmful side effect was the damage it caused to their teeth and gums. One woman came complaining of pain in her mouth. I had never seen such inflamed gums. Tiny deformed stubs of teeth were all she had left. When I gently pulled them, they all but fell out. I gave her a mouthwash to heal the infection. What more could I do for a woman who had a lifelong addiction to chewing betelnut?

A young mother was in a major crisis. She'd had her second child but the placenta had not been delivered, so they brought her to me. They had spent at least two nights in villages along the way, likely having traveled for three days. Her baby seemed healthy but the mother faced a life-threatening complication. By now the exposed cord was infested with maggots. Her friends carried her on a door for a stretcher and placed her, door and all, on my table. How could I help her?

I cried. I didn't want to do it! I feared for what might happen. How could I possibly remove the retained placenta? I couldn't send her to a hospital by plane, for that service would not be available for another 15 years. And to send them on downstream in their canoe would be sending her to her death. I would have to be brave. With God's help I might be able to release her from her distress. We prayed before I started.

Gordon sat on a stool nearby, reading to me from my obstetrics manual, describing all the things I should and should not do. The book said that to go in with an ungloved hand was safer because one could feel more accurately just what to do. I was supposed to get my fingers behind the placenta without damaging the uterine wall. And it was mandatory that I pull the whole placenta out in one piece, leaving no loose membranes behind which would cause continual bleeding and infection. I had no instruments to perform a dilatation and curettage procedure.

To keep my hand in position in her uterus was a difficult problem. Every few minutes the patient had heavy contractions as she tried to expel my hand. When she relaxed I had another few precious minutes to do what I had to do. Then she went into shock! Her family said this also happened in the last village where they had spent the night. The women there had tried to help her their way. We revived her by sprinkling cold water on her face.

Finally, I got my fingers firmly around that placenta and managed to get it out without any fragments. Thank God it was intact! I had spent hours freeing her from her dilemma. When she was brought to me, I certainly had not envisioned a success story. But God made it possible. I gave her what little antibiotic medication I had left and watched her recover. It was the most difficult medical procedure I ever performed.

The family put up a simple grass mat for a wall of protection around her on our front porch. After she recuperated her father bragged for months about how she had gotten her health back. Because of this, the community figured I could do anything! Little did they know that I would never again have the courage to tackle any internal problems, except for treating intestinal parasites and dysentery.

In July 1955 we were assigned to move to the Balai Sepuak Theological School to learn about their administrative and teaching programs. The children and I stayed at the school after conference while Gordon returned to Ambalau to pick up our household things.

While he was up there on his own, a medical emergency presented a big challenge for him. It was a case of two men and one woman in a drunken brawl. Gordon had seen them at the government office across the river and heard they would be coming to him for help. He hoped they would arrive before dark, for he only had small kerosene lamps by which to see. But no, they completed the full investigation first. The emergency treatment could wait! When they finally arrived the darkness of night had settled in.

The woman was the victim. One of the men had swung his machete and in the process had partially scalped her. Gordon shaved off her hair and at the same time removed layers of congealed blood. He cleansed the area, sutured the wound, then swabbed it with an antiseptic solution and bandaged it. That was the nearest he came to being a medical missionary.

Our work in Ambalau ended too abruptly. The actual task of meeting the spiritual needs of the people had hardly begun. There would be no resident missionary in Nanga Ambalau for another 26 years. Beginning in 1981, missionary colleagues Michael and Maureen Roark had 15 good years of evangelistic outreach in that isolated place. In their time, Mochtar and his wife, Ijah, graduates of our Immanuel Bible School in Kelansam, became strong leaders who effectively mentored their kinsmen and the workers who laboured alongside them.

* * * * * * *

In Balai Sepuak we spent a year's internship at the Bible School before going back to Canada for a year's home assignment. In November 1955 Timmy was born in Sintang, the nearest town with hospital facilities. I home-schooled Kenny and Richy. In January 1956 Kenny went to the newly opened school for missionary children in Bandung, Java, for the rest of his grade one. By mid-1956 we were on our way to conference in Bandung. From there we proceeded on to Canada, making 1955 to 1957 a transition time for our family.

When we returned to Balai Sepuak in mid-1957, it soon became apparent that the church people and their neighbours from the surrounding villages were expecting medical help. In the past, missionaries who weren't medically trained had provided medicines. We couldn't really abandon them now. Helen Hall, a fellow missionary, and I shared the work.

With Helen Hall's nursing expertise and Gordon's assistance as needed, we provided health care. For my classes at the school, I developed a health text using booklets I bought in Pontianak, adding some things that specifically met our people's needs. I gave the women and girls on our campus some basic instructions on the care and feeding of infants. I also taught other classes and helped Gordon by doing his bookkeeping. His demanding schedule of teaching, school administration and upkeep of transportation equipment more than occupied his available time. I also looked after the students' personal finances—meaning I was their banker. There really wasn't any time left to do medical work. However, the community would not understand that. So Rev. Zefanya, the Indonesian head of the school, stepped in by negotiating with the churches' elders to have two clinic days a week. Of course, emergencies didn't wait for clinic days.

A father brought his nine year-old boy to Helen Hall for help. He had been in a freak accident where a thin rattan stick had gone up his nostril. This stick still had its thorns on two sides, with the thorny spikes pointing downward. To pull it back out would make painful, bleeding gashes in his nostril. Helen was baffled, so she called me. Before I even got near him the boy screamed. He had already endured many agonizing attempts to dislodge the spiked stick. I calmed him down and sized up the situation. Then I gently inserted a small artery forceps up his nostril to stretch it. Amazingly, the stick easily came free! The boy simply gasped, "A-a-ah!" He was shocked that it had come out without extreme pain. I'm sure God gave me that idea, for I could not have figured it out myself.

A severed Achilles' tendon presented another challenge. A young boy had only a small cut just above his heel, but for his future walking ability it was a devastating accident. There had to be a way to reconnect that detached tendon. While the boy was lying on a table in my emergency room, his father stood beside him to comfort him. I gave the boy a minimum amount of anesthetic. Then with small artery forceps I pulled down the white tendon which had receded up his leg. With a second forceps I pulled the lower end of the tendon up. Overlapping the two ends, I firmly joined them using a needle and thread. Still semiconscious, the boy kept impatiently crying out, "Sudah, sudah, sudah! (It's done, it's done, it's done!)" I sprinkled sulfa crystals into the wound, sutured the epidermal skin, put a dressing on it and let him go. I told the father not to let him use that foot till the wound was well healed. For several days I changed the dressing and he was able to go home, walking.

One young man came with excruciating pain in a tooth. Someone had tried to pull his aching tooth but had only broken off the crown. It so happened that while on leave in Victoria, B.C., my dentist had given me two dental forceps. He also showed me the simplest dental procedures. I used one of those forceps, gently pushing them beyond the gum to surround the root of the broken tooth. I wiggled the painful tooth gently, just as my dentist had instructed. The offending root became dislodged from the jawbone, freeing the man of his agony. I gave him a mouthwash solution and let him go home.

For their hunting needs the local farmers often used homemade guns and homemade gunpowder. The process of making their gunpowder in a big wok over an open fire was very dangerous. If, while stirring the mixture, a small amount fell into the fire there would be an explosion. That's what happened to one man. While making his gunpowder it exploded in his face. Fortunately it was only a first-degree burn. And most fortunate of all, his eyes were not damaged. But the exploding gunpowder had seared his face, and had burned exposed parts of his chest and arms. For burn treatments I always kept a jar with bandages, which had been sterilized in heated Vaseline. That's what I applied to the charred areas, changing his dressings as necessary. In about a week the charred skin sloughed off. From underneath a layer of healthy epidermal skin appeared. He looked like a new man.

A lady came with a thorny, rattan stick in her aural canal. Since I did not want to risk stretching the aural canal, the channel to the inner ear, I cut the stick in half lengthwise with small surgical scissors. Then, guiding the thorny side away from the canal wall, I pulled it out. Likewise, I pulled out the other half and cleansed the canal with an antiseptic solution. What a relieved patient she was!

One of our students sustained a cut just over the lower knuckle of his thumb. The tendon was also severed. I was able to reconnect it so that he could regain full function of his hand. A careful suturing procedure and clean bandages was all he needed for a satisfactory recovery.

Behind the students' dormitory, during the rainy season, a little stream became a swamp. It was well named Terus Demam (or, constant fever) for it was the breeding ground for the anopheles mosquito, the carrier of malaria. This was the only mosquito that alighted on the skin at a 45-degree angle ready to sting. The female anopheles mosquitoes injected their venom while sucking up blood for procreation purposes. Those were the dangerous bloodsuckers. As I entered the students' rooms at night, I saw their mosquito nets covered with anopheles mosquitoes. It seemed that one or another person at the school was always being treated for malaria. How could one win that battle when the jungle was full of swamps during the rainy season?

One evening a student's wife had a baby. After assisting her with the delivery and checking to see that all things were in order, I left her in her husband's care, showing him how to massage the uterine area so that it would always feel like a firm, fist-sized rock. That was the sign of a firmly contracted uterus, which meant that hemorrhaging would be prevented.

About three o'clock in the morning, I was suddenly called to her room. She was lying in a pool of blood in a semiconscious state. She frequently smacked her lips, a symptom of thirst and dangerous hemorrhaging. I had no equipment to give her an intravenous solution to restore the fluid in her vascular system. My medical files gave directions to make a normal saline solution with the right amount of sugar added to supplement her blood loss. I spoon-fed a litre of this solution to her, and she revived enough to begin to take nourishment more readily.

Sadly, this couple was known among the students for their estranged and abusive relationship. Sometimes the husband spent nights away from the dormitory, sleeping in a hut by himself. Though Gordon made earnest attempts to reconcile their estrangement, the man was adamant. He did not want to be reconciled with his wife, which saddened our hearts. Eventually Gordon took them to the mouth of the main river where they could find their way on a commercial riverboat to their home village.

My next challenge was to help a boy who had fallen out of a tree. He had sustained a compound fracture with bones exposed just above his wrist. I cleansed the area, bandaged it, and fashioned a well-fitted splint to protect it. I had no equipment to make a cast. I gave him antibiotic medication, and changed the dressings for some days. Then the family decided that they had to go back to their village for more rice. As they passed through a certain hamlet, a Chinese family gave the father special advice. They said, "Take a half grown chick and pound it to a pulp—feathers, viscera and all. Use this as a poultice on the wound, and the broken bones will quickly heal." That was disastrous advice. Fresh animal dung is notorious for being contaminated with the tetanus virus.

A week later the boy was brought back. By then, the chicken poultice gave off a putrid odor. Though still walking, he had an intense, agonizing spasm about every ten minutes. I asked the father to take him to the river to remove the smelly poultice. I cleansed the washed area with an antiseptic solution and covered it with clean dressings. Any tetanus antitoxin I gave him in his advanced state of the disease would be too late to help him. All I could do was give him pain relievers.

The spasms quickly increased in frequency and intensity. In 24 hours he was dead. His was a very painful death, for in the end, his whole body was in a constant state of spasm. Since this was the only son who had been supportive and helpful at home, it was a very sad time for the father. It was also the only tetanus case I ever observed.

A man came with three fingers cut off on one hand. Only the index finger and thumb remained. Stretching the epidermal skin to cover all the muscles and subcutaneous areas, I cleansed the wound and repaired it. It healed well, and he retained the use of his index finger and thumb. Accidents caused by the careless use of machetes were common.

One of our students jumped into the river near the landing raft. Because the river was flooding he didn't see a submerged, dead tree. As he hit its branches, a two-inch splinter of hardwood entered his groin. Since it was embedded fairly deeply, he was in severe pain. A surgical procedure in this situation required a local anesthetic. Since I could feel the splinter I latched onto it with sterile artery forceps and pulled it out. Meanwhile, beside me, the friend who had brought him began feeling faint. I asked him to sit down and put his head between his knees until he recovered. Returning to the repair of the wound, which was quite small, I inserted antibiotic crystals, sutured it up and applied clean dressings. I gave him a penicillin injection to quickly heal that sensitive area.

Another student begged to go home for a Christmas visit even though he was not feeling well. Against our better judgment we gave him permission. Unfortunately, people in his village were suffering from typhus fever (an intestinal infection). In his weakened condition he became a ready victim. When he returned to the school, he suffered from a raging fever. Shortly after that, when I did a morning check, I was shocked to see on his face a deathly pallor. He was only semiconscious. His friend admitted that just that morning, during a bowel movement, he had expelled a large amount of blood. It was a crucial alarm.

With the help of several students, Gordon immediately took him to the Sanggau Government Hospital. Even with the use of the fastest boat we had, it was a 14-hour trip. On arrival, the doctor who examined him said that the patient had a 40 percent chance of survival. Back at the school our students fervently prayed for him. The young man spent many weeks in hospital. Thankfully, he did recover and was able to finish his courses for the semester.

Gordon was not content to abandon the case there. He realized that our whole school was now in danger of contracting typhus fever. He asked the doctor for serum to immunize the students and staff at our school. The doctor was reluctant to give us what we needed. His wife, who was a good friend of ours, begged him to give us some. But still he refused. Fortunately we had a colleague in Pontianak who went to the Provincial Public Health Office to get a bottle of serum. They gave him one providing we would replace it from the main Public Health Office in Bandung, Java.

Our colleague immediately took the bus from Pontianak to Sanggau, where Gordon was waiting for the serum. When Gordon returned to Balai Sepuak, I was able to immunize our student body and staff along with any villagers who wished to be protected from the dreaded disease.

The next time we were in Sanggau the doctor in the hospital confronted Gordon. He said the Provincial Health Clinic in Pontianak had asked him if there was a typhus fever epidemic in his jurisdiction. The Sanggau doctor told Gordon that he usually reported all cases such as scrub typhus so that he would not have to go up and down all the rivers in the area to immunize the village people. No, Gordon did not report him. He had merely asked for serum to immunize our Balai Sepuak Bible School families. On other occasions, I also immunized our people against Asiatic cholera and other deadly epidemic diseases.

One man came with a huge ulcer between his shoulder blades. It had obviously been there for a long time. The outer rim of the ulcer was extremely swollen and inflamed. The center of it was alive with a thick layer of maggots. The putrid smell of it was so bad that I could not clean it out in one process. What was left after that procedure was a cavity more than one inch deep and five inches across. I gave him antibiotics and cleaned the ulcer daily for several weeks. It healed well around the edges. However, since he didn't have the patience to wait for complete healing, he went home. Many months later I heard that he had died. I am not sure what caused his death.

A mother carried her 15 year-old son on her back, trekking over the jungle trails for many hours to bring him to me. He had a distended abdomen caused by an advanced case of peritonitis, an inflammation of the abdominal muscle. In my first months in registered nurses' training I had seen a similar condition caused by abdominal cancer. We had been assigned to watch the draining process. It was a timely lesson for me. For this boy I pricked a small hole on one side of his abdominal wall. Large amounts of decaying fluid flowed out. I knew immediately that I would not be able to help him recover. I could only provide some relief by draining the purulent fluid away and treating him with painkillers. That fluid probably came from a perforated bowel caused by intestinal infestations.

One of my children had itchy bites on her legs and arms that were exposed while she was asleep. I was puzzled. Then I remembered that her new mattress, filled with kapok, had been handmade in a home where the family had the common marks of chronic scabies. Fortunately, I had some strong disinfectant crystals, which I sprinkled into an empty drum. I threw the crib mattress into the drum and closed the lid tightly, leaving the mattress there for several weeks. After airing it thoroughly, it caused no more problems and was safe to use.

Since the Saturday clinic days seemed to be busier than the mid-week clinic days, I trained some of our students to help me. It was valuable experience for them, and provided much-needed assistance for me.

The wife of one of our teachers was having a baby. The first stage of delivery proceeded fairly normally but delivering the placenta was slow. Though I feared another retained-placenta problem, she eventually delivered it without my assistance. Just then, a friend of hers brought in a large bottle of warm water. Apparently it was to be used in lieu of a hot water bottle to relieve pain after her delivery.

Fortunately I was there when that happened. It became a great opportunity to give all of her female friends at the school a lesson in the danger of post-partum hemorrhaging. I showed them how to massage the uterine area till it was firm. I said that applying heat would relax the uterine muscle and cause dangerous bleeding. However, if it remained firm, she would be safe. The mother who had just delivered her baby said, "Oh, that's what happened to my sister. She died from losing too much blood!" It was an opportune time for an important lesson.

There were numerous other health needs that we treated at Balai Sepuak. But, as the years progressed, I was getting very tired and was having monthly malarial-type fevers which I could not control. Fortunately our school would be moving to Kelansam, which was on the main river where the government hospital in Sintang was upstream, a mere 45 minutes by motorboat. After we moved, when villagers still came to me for medication, I gave them a couple of aspirins and asked them to travel to the hospital in Sintang as soon as possible. At our new Kelansam Bible School campus I only provided medical care for our students and staff and their families.

In 1969, we were assigned to work in East Indonesia, teaching in cities where government health facilities were always available. By then, my nursing days were virtually over. From that time on I spent most of my time in teaching and church ministries, a change I really enjoyed.

Back in the early 1960s, a government medical clinic administrator came to Balai Sepuak. In consultation with me and our Indonesian brethren, he promised that if we would provide 100 patients a month, a medical clinic could be set up in our town. After deliberations with our regional church elders, Rev. Zefanya, the national head of our school, wrote a letter to the Provincial Health Office in Pontianak, requesting a clinic for the Belitang district. At first that service was only available sporadically and they often ran out of medications. But by the late 1970s Balai Sepuak actually had a little government hospital.

These medical cases are highlights of the jungle health services we provided in our time. How had we been able to serve the local people in holistic ways—both medically and spiritually? In Ambalau our brief work ended so abruptly that meeting the spiritual needs of people had hardly begun. However, in Balai Sepuak we, along with our colleagues and students, had ample time to share the good news of salvation in Jesus Christ on clinic days at our school, as well as during our numerous visits to the surrounding villages.

Thirty years later, infrastructures within the province have been added that have released our missionary colleagues from the many medical demands which we experienced during our time. These systems have freed them to do the more important job of training Indonesian workers to minister among their own people.

Breaking barriers—an MAF plane lifts off in Kalimantan

The Kapuas River, snaking its way through the rainforests of Borneo

CHAPTER 5

WINGS OF LOVE

Wings of Love, *Wings of Hope*, and *Flights of Mercy* are all so descriptive of Missionary Aviation Fellowship (MAF) services. Their pilots and staff make numerous ministries possible that could never be realized without their help. These airlines lighten the load for the missionaries and Indonesians and they speed the expansion of evangelistic outreach. Five-passenger single-engine Cessna planes, twin-engine planes, float planes and even helicopters used by MAF in more than 30 countries have made missionary work in remote places achievable. With increasing intertribal conflicts in many regions, MAF has become a lifeline for hundreds of thousands of refugees and the people who serve them. And when natural disasters hit, MAF is often the first to provide essential aid. That, in simplest form, describes the extent of their work.

Like the wings of eagles soaring on the wind, MAF pilots rise high above the earth, getting a clear heavenly view of where they are going. They scan the jagged mountains, the rough terrain and the rivers that snake their way through rainforest valleys and over hazardous rapids far below. They see the smoke that rises from the fires of hundreds of isolated villages, and glimpse the simple landing strips that stretch out here and there where they touch base with folks in need. People wait for them to carry their sick to the hospital, to bring in mail and needed supplies, and to transport missionaries and their Indonesian assistants to places of ministry. MAF flights remove the extreme weariness, the long lonely hours of trudging jungle trails and battling the elements on the dangerous treks to reach people. This flight service is so well illustrated in Isaiah 40:31b, "They will soar on wings like eagles; they will run and not grow weary, they will walk and not be faint."

* * * * * * *

When we arrived in West Borneo in 1953, we did all our work the hard way. Although we prayed for 15 years for MAF to be given government permission to help us, by 1968 it still had not been authorized. The first trip to our far interior station took many weeks of risky travel. MAF could have gotten us there in two and a half hours. Those were the logistics. Finally, the excellent cooperation between MAF personnel and government officials in the remote areas of the province of Papua won the day.

In 1969 we were assigned to work in Makassar, Sulawesi, East Indonesia. We went back to West Borneo to pick up our outfit, flying on MAF's first service flight from Pontianak to Sintang. I carefully buckled myself into my seat on the five-passenger plane, and gazed down at the dangerous waterways.

Looking down at those many turns in the rivers, our numerous dangerous encounters came to mind. Even with navigation maps, traveling with a motorized houseboat in the dry season was frequently a major challenge. We had been hung up on sandbars and were occasionally stuck on rocks and piles of deadwood logs lodged in the mud just below the water's surface. Sometimes we had been skilled enough to shoot the rapids. I recalled the long journeys, the isolation we experienced, the two occasions when we had been kept under house arrest in our own boat and the life-threatening episodes our family experienced during our journeys. Looking back on it all made this the most emotional one hour flight I have ever had. If only MAF services had been available during our time.

* * * * * * *

In 1953 Gordon's struggle for survival in the tempestuous waters of the Gansai Rapids near Nanga Ambalau was one of the most unforgettable events. We had settled in at our station only a few months before. A colleague transporting supplies was stuck at Gansai. To make it upstream, he needed more manpower to help him overcome the river's fierce cataract force. As a 911 call, he sent several of his crew in a rowboat to get help from Ambalau. Gordon and some friends from our neighborhood gathered ropes, paddles and long poles to help guide the stranded boat upriver. By the time they spotted the distressed vessel, the afternoon light was quickly fading. Dusk arrives early in the tropics, especially when you are surrounded by high mountains.

The men tied a rope to a strong tree above the rapids. Then the crew in the boat pulled with all their might, giving their vessel the slightest thrust forward. Some of the men used the long poles to keep the 40-foot vessel from going aground. Gordon, standing on a rock near the river's edge, was assigned to hold a rope tied to the stern of the boat to keep the vessel from being dashed on the rocks. As the rope slowly slipped through his fingers it came to its end, and he had to let go of it.

At that moment he felt the fierce power of the angry waves— a totally new experience! His feet were swept off the rock and he was pulled down, helplessly tumbling in the raging current, surfacing from time to time. Again and again he tried to grab a rock to pull himself out of danger, but his waterlogged sneakers kept dragging him into the swift, swirling waters. Because he could not swim, he became so exhausted that he just wanted to give up. There was no fear. He would go straight to heaven. But remembering his family in Ambalau, he tried one last time and managed to pull himself onto a ridge above the water. He was breathless, but he was safe. A pioneering missionary, Rev. Arthur Mouw had almost lost his life in those same rapids 28 years earlier.

The men decided to quit for the night and returned home. One of Gordon's friends rushed up the bank to tell me that my husband had almost drowned. I was stunned, but oh so grateful that he was safe. Unfortunately, he had lost his glasses in his struggle, and without them had very poor vision. One of his friends jokingly remarked that a fish was now wearing them. The next day, with a rowboat, they brought the freight to Ambalau in several trips.

Six weeks later Gordon developed a relentless fever. He remembered his experience in the rapids and felt terror. When he closed his eyes he saw dragon figures floating about over his head, hallucinatory images that taunted him to fear. When Gordon spoke the name of Jesus they vanished. In the name of His Lord, fear was dispelled and peace returned.

* * * * * *

Travel was seldom easy on the rivers so far in the interior. Surrounded by extremely high mountains and deep gorges, special navigating techniques were vital for survival in the narrow waterways. When the heavy rains came, waters in the middle of the river would actually form in a convex bow, a spectacular phenomenon. Huge logs floated downstream at a great speed. At the narrow river's edges, branches from nearby trees were actually separated from their trunks and pulled into the swift waters. Nobody in their right mind would ever try to venture out in a boat until the most dangerous flooding subsided.

On one such occasion, visiting government officials from other islands requested an immediate ride upstream to villages where they were expected to monitor the country's general election. Gordon told them the waterways were not safe. They refused to wait. He consented to take them for a test ride providing they left all their baggage behind. After a 15-minute ride upriver, with large logs speeding toward them and no space to escape, they saw the danger and were willing to wait for the fierce elements to settle. Once the worst of the flooding subsided, travel actually became safer because most of the rapids disappeared into the deeper water.

Gordon became accustomed to the dangers of traveling on the rivers, avoiding the hazards of flooding by timing his evangelism trips to the villages. He learned many lessons from the merchants who traveled on these waterways. Transporting sheets of latex they garnered from tapping rubber trees, and the highly valued resin they collected from giant virgin-forest timber, the merchants exchanged their goods for rice. Gordon also began to understand the farmers' interdependent lifestyles and their needs. But most of all, he saw the fear and the burdens they carried in their bondage to animism. Would he be able to reach them with the liberating power of Jesus Christ?

We visited villages where they traditionally feasted at the end of their harvest. The village people extended invitations to those in neighbouring hamlets. The habit-forming sirih, a combination of betel leaf, areca nut, lime and usually some tobacco leaves, had to be provided for all guests. These ingredients were pounded into a wad which they chewed for hours. This drug numbed their pain, but it also rotted their teeth and inflamed their gums.

At the feast the villagers served large amounts of cooked rice mixed with seasoned meats. The first morsels of the best food had to be presented to the evil spirits to appease them. These were carefully laid out on a banana leaf and placed on the lid of a large water jar, which carried ancestral value. Since their revelry continued for days, their meat was often spoiled before they had a chance to cook it all.

They also consumed copious amounts of rice wine. I once saw an inebriated father carrying his child in a sling on his back. I feared for the child's safety. If the father should venture from the traditional longhouse, down the steep ladder to the ground below, the child would be in danger.

After the feasting, there were long nights of drumming, dancing and drunkenness. At times it ended in brawls. We never spent the evenings with them, but from the security of our own home we could hear the beat of their drumming all night long. As the night wore on the drums beat faster and faster ending at dawn in a frightening frenzy. By their dancing incantations they were trying to appease the numerous spirits they feared. What a hopeless life! They received no relief from the spirits and they depleted their rice holdings, which should have been their food for the whole year.

Feasts for the dead also required generous amounts of food, freely provided for all neighbours who attended. For the cause, they sacrificed their limited number of domestic animals. A fully feathered live rooster was dipped in the blood of those animals, and then committed to the spirits of their gods to invoke their blessing. After that, the blood was sprinkled on all who attended, which was supposed to protect them from harm. If only they knew of the blood of Jesus which could free them from their bondage of sin and fear! This blood ceremony became a bridge to teach them about the power of Christ's blood, which was shed to cleanse them from sin and to release them from the fears of the powers of evil spirits.

Likewise, at wedding ceremonies, blood collected in a bowl was first sprinkled on the bride and groom and then on all who attended. They hoped it would protect them from evil spirits. Then the bridal pair went to stand in the shallows of a river where they were covered with a fishing net. With incantations to symbolize their union, they were pronounced husband and wife. This ceremony was always preceded by a well-planned sirih ritual between the parents of the bride and the groom. That ritual committed the bridal pair to look after either the groom's parents or the bride's parents when they became disabled in their elderly years, an old-age security system that bound the generations together.

* * * * * * *

You've got mail! Every three months we would get a sack full of mail. Between mail deliveries, we received no other news except for what was broadcasted from FEBC in Manila. Even telegrams could not reach us in our very remote village. As we dumped the volume of mail on our living room floor, we would pick out the first class mail and digest its contents for days. Later, we sifted through the rest.

When Gordon was away for weeks at a time on evangelistic trips in the villages, the isolation for me and our two little boys was especially difficult. We had to commit ourselves to our Father's keeping. However, beginning in our first weeks in Ambalau, medical work kept me busy as I looked after the sick that came to our door.

* * * * * * *

Without MAF, going to our first field conference in Java was a major challenge. It took about three months to travel there, attend the conference and return again to our remote village. Having only a canoe, we depended on river merchants for long distance travel. By then, Gordon realized that we would need to save all the money possible to buy our own motorized boat. In the meantime, he asked our neighbour to take us to the nearest merchant town down river.

Merchant barge traveling the Kapuas River

Arriving there, we discovered that riots which were instigated by villagers from surrounding areas had devastated the merchants' livelihood. The merchants had taken their outboard motors and travel equipment to a safer place, a full day's journey downriver. We wondered how we would find a way to travel downstream.

Because it was the dry season, commercial river barges, which usually provided some space for travelers, would not be navigating upriver for many weeks to come. Several schoolboys were also waiting for passage. We rented a 20-foot rowboat and hired the boys to row us downriver where we could connect with a commercial vessel. First, the boys decided to construct a simple roof. We bought roofing material made of palm branches. They tied poles to the inside of the boat to secure the roofing. That gave us some shelter from the sun. Unfortunately, a rainstorm hit and nearly blew the roof away, giving us very little protection from the drenching downpour.

It took a while to find lodging after that storm. Not all riverside merchants were willing to give us the space. By the time we finally found a shopkeeper who would give us accommodation in his landing raft, our two boys were fast asleep on wet blankets. It was Kenny who got chilled. Before we got to the next merchant town of Nanga Pinoh his body was becoming limp with a fever. Fortunately, there was a clinic where Catholic nuns gave us medication for his serious throat infection. It took a week for him to recover.

After more delays we were able to get passage on a commercial river barge with limited cabin space. It would take about ten more days to get to the port city of Pontianak. Oh, how we longed for MAF services. Upon arrival in Pontianak we had to wait for plane space to get to Jakarta, where other missionaries would meet us. Then, at the first opportunity we took the four-hour drive by bus to Bandung where our conference was held. What we really needed at that point was a long rest. Instead we were immediately thrust into the busyness of meetings and deliberations.

After the conference we returned to Pontianak and sailed upstream to Balai Sepuak with our missionary colleagues. The boys and I stayed there for several months while Gordon traveled upstream to Ambalau. When he returned in mid-September we borrowed the mission houseboat for a temporary home to travel upriver to the government hospital in Sintang, where we awaited the arrival of baby Kathy. After her safe birth, I was confined to bed for three weeks with post-partum thrombo-phlebitis. Because of the complications of my confinement, we finally did have a pseudo-family vacation.

Finally ready to go home, we took a commercial river barge to its terminal point in Nanga Serawai. It would take another four hours by outboard motorboat to get to Ambalau. Gordon sent a message to our Chinese neighbor in Ambalau to please come and get us. The message took about a week to reach him. Meanwhile, a kind storekeeper gave us lodging in his landing raft at the edge of the river. It was comfortably clean and had two rooms. We set up our camping equipment and prepared to cook our meals and wait. Baby Kathy spent most of her time sleeping in her bassinet.

But for five year-old Kenny and four year-old Richy, being confined to the landing raft was difficult. They watched the village children swimming at the river's edge. Not having learned to swim yet, they stood on the ledge on the outside of our landing raft, vicariously enjoying the children's fun. When suddenly it was too quiet I rushed out to see if the boys were okay. Gordon came out right after me. Alarmed, Kenny said as he pointed to a two-foot square hole in the ledge, "Richy fell in!" Just at that moment Gordon glimpsed Richy's blonde hair floating just below the water's surface. He plunged his hand in and grabbed him, managing to pull him to safety through that small hole in the floor before the river carried him away. What a relief to pull him to safety so quickly!

Children playing on a *lanting* (landing raft)

We realized immediately that Richy having been rescued at all was a miracle. Our landing raft was on the upstream end of many landing rafts moored side-by-side. If he had surfaced anywhere else, he could have drifted underwater from landing raft to landing raft, never being able to get his head above water. It would have taken an experienced swimmer who was familiar with such a crisis to save himself.

There we stood. We were all so shaken. Fortunately Richy hadn't yet swallowed any of the dirty water. His face was a deathly pallor, and he had great blue circles around his eyes. All he said was, "The water is so yellow!" With embracing affection we talked at length about the miraculous deliverance, and together thanked our God for rescuing him from a watery grave.

Paul spoke of such a crisis in II Corinthians 1:10-11, "He has delivered us from such a deadly peril, and He will deliver us. On Him we have set our hope that He will continue to deliver us, as you help us by your prayers. Then many will give thanks on our behalf for the gracious favour granted us in answer to the prayers of many." How thankful we were for family and friends in the homeland who prayed for our safety. Their prayers formed a crucial lifeline. Heaven will reveal how many times we were delivered because of the prayers of those who continually remembered us.

* * * * * * *

Kathy also had an experience she will never forget when she was five years old. We were scheduled to go on a business trip to Singapore. Gordon was taking Kathy and Timmy to stay with the John Van Patters in Nanga Pinoh. Gordon moored the two mission launches at the mouth of the Kayan River where he was dropping off students after their year of schooling. Other students would also go to Nanga Pinoh to find a way home to their villages. I stayed back at our station to clear up many loose ends after the school year and to make preparations for our next trip.

Our boats, along with many others, were moored side-by-side at the river's edge. While minding our children, some of the girls on one boat were busy washing clothes and others were preparing food for the day. Timmy had fun watching them and Kathy wanted to join her kid brother. But she was on another boat. A gangplank made a good catwalk between the boats. Why not walk across it like everybody else did? She tried, but suddenly lost her footing and plunged into the swift current of the flooding river. Rumpa, a skilled student in managing dangerous waters, heard her fall in and immediately dove in after her and pulled her to safety. If Kathy had not been rescued quickly she could have been trapped, for the flooding Kayan River, pouring its waters into the main river, activated a swift, swirling undercurrent. It was a miraculous rescue for one frightened little girl! The trauma of that experience stayed with her for a long time.

Since our homes in Kalimantan were always near a river, and since we continually traveled on rivers, one of the fears I lived with every day was the safety of our children.

* * * * * * *

In the early 1960s, when Communism became a real threat, being held up at one or more of the many checkpoints along the river was a continuing nightmare. Once, with our children on board, we were held under house arrest in our own houseboat. We didn't know how long we would be confined. We were puzzled, for as far as we knew we had done nothing wrong. Fortunately, it lasted only 24 hours. A security advisor who knew us traveled overland through the night to investigate the problem. The interaction was amiable. The reason for our detention proved to be a lack of information between different government departments. With MAF services we would have avoided the delay by flying nonstop right to our destination.

In November 1962, Gordon picked up our school-aged children at the port city of Pontianak. They were coming home for the Christmas vacation. Sylvia, just over a year old, and I waited upcountry for their arrival. When they were late returning, we thought that perhaps the boats were in trouble, or that perhaps there had been an accident. We had no way of getting word from them. The radio broadcast from Manila that Saturday morning mentioned President Kennedy's assassination. That news only added to my anxiety.

On the tenth day, with no word of where they were, I took the day off, packed a simple lunch and Sylvia and I walked a short distance into the jungle where we could be alone together. Sylvia played with a few toys beside me while I sat on a log to meditate and pray. The next morning we walked through the woods to the nearest Sunday church service. About half way into our return journey, I suddenly saw a blonde boy running up the path to meet us. It was Timmy! Our children were home! I was overwhelmed with joy.

Why were they ten days late? They had been traveling with two mission launches when both motors broke down. At that point, they approached a missionary friend's home who lived near the river. This friend had the tools to do the repairs on their motors. What better place to stop to do the job! Other dependable mechanics were only available 18 hours travel back downstream in Pontianak. As soon as one launch's motor was repaired, our colleagues Bill and Jan Kuhns were able to bring our children home. After the second motor was repaired, Gordon followed with the other launch.

* * * * * * *

These were just some of the memories that filled my mind that day in 1969 as we flew on the first MAF service flight from Pontianak to Sintang. If we could have had this service during our 15 years of ministry in West Borneo, we would have avoided many delays and stressful days of river travel. Most of all, we would have prevented the hazardous, life-threatening events my family experienced. Again and again our faithful Deliverer had snatched us all from the jaws of death. Those were poignant rescues. Could anyone deny the incredible benefits of MAF mercy flights?

Church meeting held in a temporary chapel in Kelansam. John Van Patter is seated at centre. Richard Chapman is on the right. second row.

CHAPTER 6

A PERPETUAL HARVEST

Sowing and reaping, planting and harvesting is common terminology the world over. Jesus often used that metaphor as an illustration in his teaching, speaking of planted seeds that produce new life. In nature, seeds that are planted die before new life is born. Likewise, "… as in Adam all die, so in Christ all will be made alive." (I Corinthians 15:22) Through Adam's fall we were born in sin and faced an eternal separation from God. However, God graciously provided a new life—life that needs daily renewal in the Spirit. "Therefore, if anyone is in Christ, he is a new creation …" (II Corinthians 5:17) That is the continually-renewed life that God expects us to pass on. His life is the most precious heritage that we could ever hand down to succeeding generations. In His fervent concerns for the disciples in John 17:20, Christ added, "My prayer is not for them alone. I pray also for those who will believe in me through their message, … " That is the essence of God's plan for perpetuating a harvest—sowing, watering and reaping—until the end of time.

Jesus gave us the compelling mandate in Matthew 9:37-38, "Then saith he unto his disciples, 'The harvest truly is plenteous, but the labourers are few; Pray ye therefore the Lord of the harvest, that he will send forth labourers into his harvest.'" (KJV) At the Balai Sepuak Bible School in West Borneo, we had our first opportunity to prepare labourers for a spiritual harvest in Indonesia.

But the job description was daunting. Filling the roles of teacher, preacher, mechanic, builder, administrator, counselor, arbitrator and motivator presented a challenge. Previously one or another of our missionary colleagues had served the community in these areas. Were we obligated to do all they had done? How could we possibly fulfill all these expectations? More importantly, what was God expecting us to do? We'd had no training in some of these skills; we certainly weren't qualified to do them. It would be an on-the-job education. First and foremost, we would have to learn to understand the culture of our people and our physical environment. We made numerous mistakes. Thankfully many of our dear Indonesian brethren loved us in spite of our blunders.

To train Indonesian Christians to reach their kinsmen was most important. This responsibility is reiterated in the Apostle Paul's words in II Timothy 2:2, "And the things you have heard me say in the presence of many witnesses entrust to reliable men who will also be qualified to teach others." That is the core emphasis of the "perpetual harvest" in Kingdom work.

In 1960 Gordon reported, "The continuing advance of the work of God upon the solid foundation of the Word of God is the principle enunciated in the above words. It is the burden of our hearts to impart the truths of Scripture to faithful men. We were thankful for faithful students who were preparing for the Lord's work. They often made up in faithfulness for what was lacking in educational advantage. We were gratified by their progress and good attitudes."

Since we'd had only six months of learning the Indonesian language when we started, we didn't feel linguistically skilled to teach. In those early days, most of our students in Balai Sepuak had only completed the elementary level of education in their national language. Therefore, we would be learning together. That didn't seem to be a problem. We actually learned by contending with obstacles and we improved in our language skills as we prepared teaching materials.

A big problem for Gordon was having to attend committee meetings in Java related to field administration matters. For example, during the 1959/60 school year, he was absent for 100 days. That was not in the best interest of our students. Two Indonesian teachers and four single missionary teachers had to teach the classes he missed. His departure was delayed by disciplinary crises that arose at the last minute. And, as Gordon said, together with the Indonesian teachers I had to manage many of the issues that surfaced in his absence. Without exception, divine wisdom and constant vigilance were indispensable.

Maintaining the motors of mission launches was another problem that added stress. It wasn't just a matter of checking the fuel and oil levels. Often there were mechanical problems that had to be corrected before departing on another trip. Being a mechanic was not one of Gordon's interests. In fact, before we left Canada for the Far East, we hadn't even owned a car. Gordon managed by ordering mechanics' repair manuals and doing repairs himself, by the book—a demanding and time-consuming job. In the same way, he repaired the outboard motors which were used for our shorter trips and for students' travels to distant villages for evangelistic ministries. Since the rivers were our highways, we couldn't go very far without boats. However, trekking through the jungle to the various churches for weekend and special holiday ministries was often a better option.

Several villages in our district had never been reached with the gospel. In fact, their chiefs had rejected the visits of our student teams. Then a change came. A zealous young Christian named Asan had shared the good news of Jesus' salvation by word and by lifestyle. He was engaged to be married to a girl from

One of many dear Dyak friends

another village. But before leaving his home compound he requested a visit from our school. A team of students along with an accompanying teacher were delighted to follow up on this timely invitation. That visitation opened the door to another village who also wanted to hear the good news about Jesus' power to save them from sin and the bondages of fear in their animistic religion. Praise God, in both villages a number of people accepted Jesus as Saviour on that first visit. As continuing visits were made, more people wanted to follow the Jesus way. Those who were physically able attended the nearest church fellowship meetings. That was a great encouragement for all of us at the school.

About once a month, students went home on weekends to get their rice. It gave them an opportunity to serve in their home churches in practical ministry. During the school's long vacation each student was expected to serve half of the time in Christian service, preferably in non-Christian villages. That assignment depended on the cooperation of their pastors. Some enthusiastic pastors actually left their ministry in the hands of their lay leaders for a weekend so that they could visit people who had never heard the news of salvation in Jesus.

A big need for our Indonesian teachers at the school was their daily rice supply. They were desperate. Pastors in the district got their rice from their parishioners. Our teachers had no such assistance. For lack of time they couldn't plant their own rice fields. And students' incomes were too limited to help pay for all of the Indonesian teachers' living expenses. Then our Mission devised a plan to put them on subsidies. Improvements were made in that subsidy plan when Rev. Kamasi came as a speaker from the Jaffray Theological College in Makassar for the Kelansam Bible School graduation in May 1967. He spoke of Jaffray College's system of paying teachers' wages based on the local price of rice. This plan would pay for their food as well as for other living expenses. Not until near the end of the 20th century would students find additional opportunities to earn extra money, and in their school fees help to finance the teachers' living expenses.

* * * * * * *

In the mid-1950s the school administration began to schedule a day of prayer once a month. As together we sought God's face, great blessing came to many students and teachers. Our students were most deeply affected by our Indonesian leader, Rev. Zefanya, whose sermons were clearly spoken in their heart language. Gordon recorded one of his last messages. After Rev. Zefanya's untimely death, that message was played during a day of prayer. An amazing move of God came over the assembly. It was a voice from beyond the grave, spoken by a man they loved.

Rev. Zefanya, the head at the school for at least five of our years in Balai Sepuak, had a passionate love for God. Often he acted as a peacemaker between workers in the area, between the school and the community, between students on campus, and between government officials and the missionaries. How we would miss his wise counsel and spiritual maturity when we returned after furlough in 1962. With his sudden death our advocate was gone.

He hadn't always lived in complete victory. One evening he came to see us because he wanted me to be an advisor in his home. Because of discord in his marriage relationship he didn't feel worthy to be the leader of the school. As both husband and wife shared at length I talked with them about some of the reasons for their hurtful feelings. I encouraged them to have a daily devotional time together and to verbally pray for each other. Then in concentrated prayer we committed it all to God. As a result of this time of counseling, they were able to work more closely together and God continued to bless them in ministry.

On another occasion, a letter signed by most of the male students had been sent to the district superintendent, requesting that a certain Indonesian teacher be removed. In this case the Indonesian district leader handed that letter to my husband, asking him to be the arbitrator. He was supposed to "pull the coals out of the fire".

For some weeks Gordon quietly carried a little black book, listing students' infractions. (In their bitterness they actually rebelled more and more against school rules.) Finally on a Saturday morning he called a meeting. Sentence by sentence he read the letter the students had written, then asked if the teacher's removal was what they had intended. Most of the fellows acknowledged that it was. Several stated they hadn't taken part in the protest. Then Gordon pulled out his little black book to read what he had observed since their letter had been given to him. They were speechless! They wondered how they could have been so blind to their own faults. It was a major breakthrough. One of those students packed up and left. Several years later he did return to finish school, and became a strong evangelist and a reliable Christian worker. In the end, many of the protesting students became faithful leaders in the national church.

However, more and more churches faced issues of immorality among their young people. And middle-aged couples openly sought divorce and remarriage to solve their problems. It was a disturbing trend. There were also failings in the district leadership to deal with moral issues. A long-time faithful leader in our region decided to take time out "to tend to his family needs". He became a merchant and eventually totally backslid into the ways of the world. We and many of our friends prayed passionately for him.

How we longed to see him fully yielded to Christ! Some years later he did return to the Lord.

Another leader in an upstream synod, who was a respected and wise director, developed ulterior motives. He conducted the district conference without any devotional times and initiated a spirit of dissension among the Indonesian workers in the province. He was also quite sick with a debilitating disease. Despite John Van Patter's trekking overland a great distance to take medication for his illness, it did not help the leader. Just prior to the next provincial church conference he suddenly died. Rev. Zefanya reported that his death prevented a major split within the district. Oh, how we needed a revival! We prayed so passionately for changes to come. The work continued in a vulnerable state and we felt so helpless in coping with it. At that time someone sent us a recorded song that became a touchstone for encouragement. It was based on Ephesians 4:7, "But unto every one is given grace according to the measure of the gift of Christ." (KJV) Whenever I hear this song sung now it still evokes deep emotion:

He giveth more grace when the burdens grow greater;
He sendeth more strength when the labours increase.
To added affliction He addeth His mercy;
To multiplied trials His multiplied peace.

When we have exhausted our store of endurance,
When our strength has failed e're the day is half done,
When we reach the end of our hoarded resources,
Our Father's full giving has only begun.

Refrain:
His love has no limit; His grace has no measure;
His power has no boundary known unto men.
For out of His infinite riches in Jesus,
He giveth, and giveth, and giveth again.

—Annie J. Flint,
—Refrain: Hubert Mitchell

No Christian can overcome the continuing tests of confrontation unless there are frequent renewal experiences under the anointing of the Holy Spirit. Thankfully, in all these experiences, there were workers and students from various areas who remained faithful to God.

Encouragement also came from a Kayan River area synod, about 20 hours travel upstream by boat from the Belitang district, where the Bible School was located. The Kayan students were diligent, making every effort to work their way through school. Many became caring pastors. However, the beginnings of God's work in this area had not begun until 1953 when God opened the door for a Kingdom harvest under the evangelistic ministry of Rev. Jafet. He faithfully presented God's Word to his fellow Indonesians. At first Christians met on the verandas of their longhouses. Before long, four villages built their own churches. In 1960 Rev. Bill Kissell helped them organize a camp meeting, attracting about 700 people.

Preparing a Dyak Christmas feast of wild boar

The following year they held another conference for three days. The Christians fed 1,200 people from 35 villages, using 2 tons of rice, 33 pigs and 4 cows! They had early morning prayer meetings, children's meetings, sports for the youth, and well-attended evening meetings. On opening night the hosts, Pastor Zakaria, a chief elder and a village chief, welcomed their guests, exhorting them regarding conduct during the camp. They said, "We are glad to welcome many unbelievers to our conference. But we want you to know that ours is a Christian village, and you will be expected to conduct yourselves in proper manner. Please leave our girls alone; drinking and gambling will not be allowed; and absolute quiet is expected during the services." Their guests took the exhortation well and observed the rules. For the first time many heard the powerful gospel message presented in a Christian atmosphere.

In later years one of their men, named Wilson Ayub, who grew up in a Christian home in one of their villages, followed the good example of his father. Wilson was still young when his father took Christian lay-training classes taught by missionaries. When Wilson finished high school he studied at the Pontianak Theological College. In connection with that training he did his internship in a Pontianak city church. In 1998 he was assigned to take graduate studies in Jaffray Theological College in Makassar. Because of his good grades and excellent deportment he became a recipient of the "Gordon Chapman Memorial Scholarship". Upon returning to Pontianak he was assigned to teach at his alma mater.

On the other hand, some of the Christians in the Belitang district, who had become believers a generation earlier, were becoming indifferent towards Christianity, setting a poor example for our students. Part of the problem was that pastors often lacked incentive to study for their messages, and many neglected to visit the Christians in their villages during the week. How we prayed for a change! Our two younger missionaries, Lela Pierce and Helen Hall, began holding daily Bible classes in each church, for two weeks, especially geared towards the young people. They also held classes for children in the afternoons and where possible conducted evening services for everyone. After a year they taught similar classes in all other districts. Their teaching changed the Dyaks' appreciation for the values of the Christian life.

* * * * * * *

At our Balai Sepuak Bible School, Lela Pierce began monthly missionary meetings on Friday evenings. On the first Friday she presented a biographical study of the famous evangelist, Bak Singh. Later, when missionary colleagues visited, they were surprised to hear about "boxing" (Bak Singh) meetings! In another of her monthly meetings Lela reported on Christian youth activities in Cambodia. In her mind a vision was born. "If Cambodian young people can schedule youth meetings, so can we."

When plans for an annual youth camp were developing, Lela and Helen realized that they needed the Indonesian pastors' approval. They initiated a consultation with the pastors and received permission to proceed. But would youth be willing to attend meetings and activities from Monday to Friday? The answer soon became clear. The first year 85 young people came to enjoy a full schedule of morning meetings, games in the afternoon and evangelistic services in the evening. Many of them received Christ as Saviour. The next year 250 young people attended. The youth camp became an effective outlet to reach young people in the district.

With Helen and Lela planning for their year of home service in North America, the Indonesian pastors and young people took on the responsibility of organizing the annual event. As a result, young people who entered Bible School often shared that they had accepted Christ as Saviour at a youth camp. Only the Lord knows the full impact these camps had on all who attended. When the school moved to the Kelansam campus, a student youth committee was organized to look after the arrangements and oversee the successful operation of the camps.

* * * * * * *

To strengthen the congregations in the Belitang district, Rev. Wesley Brill, C&MA field director, held meetings for three to four days in a number of churches, resulting in good renewal experiences. Shortly after that, Rev. Germann Edy's visit presented a challenging voice from another mission. The message deeply moved Rev. Lombok, who was his interpreter. Previously Rev. Lombok had been approached by the department head of the Office of Religion in the city of Pontianak to accept a position on staff. But Rev. Germann Edy's messages persuaded him to change his mind. He remained faithful in his upcountry district ministry.

During the 1963/64 school year, we considered our visits to the Hebron, Betesda, Siloam, Galilea, Maranatha, Immanuel and Kedembak churches a very important ministry. They invited us to conduct communion, to baptize 60 new believers and to perform marriages. On these trips students always assisted us.

In the district churches, the missionaries, Indonesian teachers and our students provided special Christmas messages. Even our most senior missionaries, Lillian Marsh and Margaret Kemp, trekked the difficult trails to do their part. Lillian and Margaret were our "veterans" who had suffered unbelievably in concentration camps during the Japanese occupation of Indonesia during World War II. In spite of life-threatening experiences, they never really talked about those internment days. They willingly came back to teach at the Balai Sepuak Bible School, sharing their deep love for Christ. Revelation 22:12 speaks of their rewards, "Behold, I am coming soon! My reward is with me, and I will give to everyone according to what he has done."

Our children joined us in Christmas visits to village churches. Sometimes they shared in music as they did in the Belitang District Maranatha Church and in the Sintang Church. Through the children we could sometimes touch people who were otherwise very much on the fringes of Christianity. On one occasion Gordon and the two older boys went to one church while I and the younger three children served in another one, telling the marvels of the Christmas story.

* * * * * * *

But there was no purpose in laborious perseverance for us and our Indonesian and missionary colleagues, unless the alumni who had been trained in West Borneo became a part of the perpetual harvest to keep the church growing. Praise God they did. And the church has been growing, since we all stood together to *embrace the mountain* for the Kingdom of God. Growth over the years has been phenomenal.

In the large Immanuel Church in the Sintang regency city, Rev. Zakius Saloh, one of our alumni, has developed a large congregation where many of his students are young people who have come from their villages to study in high school. Zakius's son, Hendry, graduate of the Pontianak Theological College, is an assistant pastor. Zakius has also had an effective ministry teaching Theological Education by Extension (TEE) in Balai Agas, a fair sized town upriver.

When we left in 1967 there were about 50 students in the Immanuel Bible School in Kelansam. In the year 2000 the school had an initial record attendance of 200 students. For the past several years some students have had major victories as they have been released from occult powers. Rev. Iskandar, superintendent of the Melawi district, has been influential in sending many young people to the Immanuel Bible School. Some of them later became pastors and evangelists in the new work in the neighbouring province of Central Borneo. Other West Borneo alumni, who studied in the national church colleges in other provinces, have returned to West Borneo and are diligently planting churches upcountry.

When we relocated the Bible School to Kelansam, the Belitang district missed the school in Balai Sepuak so much that they started another school there. During part of its existence Rev. Simeon Sura, one of our former students, was its director. In 1999 they rejoiced to have a record attendance of 80 students.

Our family home in Kelansam during the 1960s

A record number of 200 students enrolled in the Pontianak Theological College in the year 2000. These students will supply the growing demand for workers in the provincial capital of 400,000 people, and will provide workers for the needs of Christian leaders in upcountry posts. Director Ibrahim Jawing's staff is mostly made up of alumni who originally studied in West Borneo, and later added graduate studies at Jaffray Theological College in Makassar. One of their professors was also given a mission scholarship to study abroad.

The population in the port city of Pontianak is growing rapidly. In 1991, the Ekklesia first national GKII (The Gospel Tabernacle of Indonesia) congregation had a burden to make an impact on this city and its suburbs. They set a goal of planting four new churches in four suburbs by the year 2000. That plan gave birth to the 4-4-2 Evangelistic Program, encouraging its members to actively participate. Though they encountered many problems, their goals were met by showing faithfulness to God and love toward those who opposed them. For example, by May 2000, the Ekklesia congregation was once again willing to release 100 people from its 600 member congregation to begin a fifth church planting. That's how Pontianak has been reaping a harvest.

Furthermore, with the help of MAF, Theological Education by Extension (TEE) has become a great influence in strengthening the churches throughout the province. TEE is a program in which instructors travel to churches, teaching theological education to laymen in various districts. Participants of these courses often become Sunday school teachers, evangelists and assistants to pastors. And frequently, because of TEE, they later pursue theological training in one of the provincial Bible schools.

MAF also assists students in ministering to villages where people haven't ever heard the good news of salvation in Jesus Christ. For instance, on the Easter long weekend in April 2001, MAF flew 47 evangelistic teams of students and teachers to numerous churches and outposts.

These stories give evidence to the "sowing and harvesting" effect of the growing church in West Borneo. The message has been carried from generation to generation, touching people who long for righteousness and peace. Acts 16:5 is so relevant, "So the churches were strengthened in the faith and grew daily in numbers." And growth continues as Christian leaders in Bible schools and churches lead people throughout the province to follow the exhortation given in Hosea 10:12, "Sow for yourselves righteousness, reap the fruit of unfailing love, and break up your unploughed ground; for it is time to seek the Lord, until he comes and showers righteousness on you."

Students attending the Kelansam Bible School, June 1966

CHAPTER 7

<u>FIRST-PERSON ACCOUNTS</u>

One of Franklin Graham's touchstone letterheads stated: "No greater task. No greater joy." Acts 20:24 verifies the pre-eminent purpose of the task, "However, I consider my life worth nothing to me, if only I may finish the race and complete the task the Lord Jesus has given me—the task of testifying to the gospel of God's grace." That conviction is the divine appointment our alumni felt so deeply. Psalm 149:4-5 confirms their anticipated joy, "For the Lord takes delight in his people; he crowns the humble with salvation. Let the saints rejoice in this honor and sing for joy … " As they followed God's plan they were truly filled with the Lord's joy. It gratified us to see many of our students become devoted servants for God. The following testimonies are examples of how God prepared them to participate in Christ's Kingdom in West Borneo.

Rev. Dimianus Simson, son of a Belitang district pastor wrote:

I became a Christian when Rev. Elmer Warkentine, of the Ansang Bible School in West Borneo, was a guest speaker at the Balai Sepuak Bible School. Rev. Warkentine and his team sang songs that overwhelmingly drew me to accept Jesus as my Saviour. Then in 1965 I got a scholarship to study for government service at the Tanjongpura University in Pontianak. But my most enjoyable times were spent as youth pastor of the GPKB Elim Church. I also served as an elder at Elim Church while I studied in Pontianak.

Later, while working on staff at the Serukam General Hospital, I had a deep longing to study in a theological school. I was so overcome with that longing that I asked the Lord to deliver me from that passion if it wasn't His will. But as I wept, my burdens merely increased. God was calling me to serve Him full-time. Finally, in 1980 to 1983, I was able to study at Jaffray Theological College in Makassar, Indonesia.

When I returned to West Borneo, I was assigned to pastor churches in Nanga Pinoh and in Pontianak from 1983 to 1988. While in Pontianak I was also chosen by the GKII (C&MA) national church to become the district superintendent of our West Borneo churches. Simultaneously, I also became director of the Pontianak Theological College.

In 1988 I received a scholarship to study at the Alliance Biblical Seminary in Manila, Philippines. When I returned to Indonesia I again served as district superintendent of the West Borneo churches, and taught part-time at the Pontianak Theological College. People told me I was working like I was "paying a debt!" [an Indonesian proverb]. In fact, I am paying a debt to my Lord who saved me. I find great joy in it.

Speaking of my teachers, I benefited by Rev. Gordon Chapman's classes because he was so creative. He seemed to be able to answer all our questions. He was a very disciplined man. Those are the most memorable lessons I learned from him.

Respectfully,
Rev. Diminaus Simson, Pontianak, October 8, 1999

* * * * * * *

Rev. Simon Enggah, a long-time friend and colleague in ministry wrote:

I became a Christian in 1948 when the songs the Christians sang drew me to faith in God. Then in 1953 I started studying at the Balai Sepuak Bible School because I wanted to serve my Lord. I served churches in Bukit Zaitun and Hebron in the Belitang district from 1955 to 1961. Then I studied at Jaffray Theological College in Makassar for two years. In 1964 I was assigned to teach at Immanuel Bible School in Kelansam, West Borneo.

[In 1965 Rev. Simon Enggah became the first National Director of Immanuel Bible School, taking over the administration from Gordon. It was a very amiable transition. We enjoyed warm fellowship with him for another two years. We found Simon to be a man of deep faith and admirable integrity—a man who was totally dedicated to God. –a.c.]

From 1978 to 1983, I served in the Getsemani and Bukit Zaitun Churches again. Since 1984 I have been back teaching at my alma mater, lecturing on the book of Daniel and Christian ethics. I have now served God for 41 years without a break. I want my life to continue to be a strong spiritual influence to the younger generation. I hope they will faithfully bring many people to believe in Jesus as they work to advance the growth of Christ's Kingdom.

Even though I am now officially retired and my strength is waning, I still manage to walk to church at Eben Haizer. [With painful arthritis, he manages this 40-minute walk. –a.c.] Please pray for me that I will always be a spiritual influence as I teach young people.

With love and prayers from our family,
Rev. Simon Enggah, Balai Sepuak, November 23, 1999

* * * * * * *

Rev. Yoel Ungking, son of a long-time elder in the Belitang district wrote:

My wife Bikas and I were deeply influenced by the Chapmans in their teaching in the Balai Sepuak Bible School, at Immanuel Bible School in West Borneo as well as at Jaffray Theological College in Makassar, Sulawesi. Their counseling was very dear to our hearts. Being taught to be thrifty, to buy good books and to study them became the foundation for our lives.

After we graduated from Immanuel Bible School in 1967 we served in pastoral ministries in the Pauh Village, in the Kayan district and at the Immanuel Church in the Belitang district. Then I was assigned to be district superintendent of the Belitang district. In 1979 to 1982, I was given a scholarship to study at Jaffray Theological College in Makassar. When I returned to West Borneo I was assigned to be teacher and director of Immanuel Theological School in Kelansam. From 1988 to the present I have been teaching at the Theological College in Pontianak in West Borneo.

We appreciated Rev. and Mrs. Chapman's advice. They were always forthright and sincerely showed us the true Christian way. Since they were so openly candid with us we accepted them as our real parents. They taught us to live disciplined, balanced Christian lives and to trust in God for our ministry.

A verse that became our life motto is one Rev. Chapman used in a message on Joshua 24:14-15, "Now fear the Lord and serve him with all faithfulness. ... As for me and my household, we will serve the Lord." That commitment is ever before us.

Sincerely,
Rev. Yoel and Mrs. Bikas Ungking, June 20, 1999

* * * * * * *

Rev. Ibrahim Jawing wrote:
From my theological training I was personally challenged to strengthen my spiritual growth. I was taught to improve my general knowledge and gain an understanding of the basics of theology for church ministries. In fact, these studies influenced me to commit my whole life to serve my Lord.

I am thankful that the congregation I served accepted the spiritual direction I gave them. And ultimately my theological training enabled me to teach my students to become spiritually qualified servants in God's Kingdom. [In 1980, after graduating from Jaffray Theological College in Makassar, the West Borneo synod elected Rev. Ibrahim Jawing to become the Director of the Pontianak Theological College. God has given him divine courage and wisdom to manage this assignment. –a.c.]

My Bible College training prepared me to be a disciplined, hard-working servant. I want to be a responsible leader for my Lord. I realize that everything I have received in knowledge, in teaching skills and in Christian character development has prepared me to catch the vision of God's purpose for the work of His Kingdom.

My goal for the GKII (C&MA) national church in West Borneo is that the good news of the gospel will bring many people to believe in Jesus as Saviour in our province. I am thankful for guidance received from Rev. and Mrs. Chapman and all my teachers.

Respectfully submitted,
Rev. Ibrahim Jawing, June 20, 1999.

* * * * * * *

Rev. Natanael Semuel, second generation pastor and Bible school teacher, wrote:
My mother had a strong influence on me in my childhood. When she taught me Bible stories I was led to become a

Christian. At that time my father was the pastor of the GKII (C&MA) Eben Haizer Church in the Belitang district of West Borneo. My mother said that I had been very ill as a child. In fact, I was so ill that there was little hope for my recovery. But the Lord intervened and I was healed.

Then my mother urged me to give my life to Christ for full-time service. When I did that I was strengthened in God's word, especially Philippians 4:11 and 13, "I am not saying this because I am in need, for I have learned to be content whatever the circumstances. ... I can do everything through Him who gives me strength." I willed to trust God in times of plenty as well as in times of need. The Lord would give me strength in everything that happened to me.

I was given a scholarship to study at Jaffray Theological College in Makassar. [In fact, Jaffray College twice named Rev. Natanael Semuel the honorary student of the year, because no other scholar had exceeded his quality of Christian deportment and academic excellence at that time. –a.c.]

When I returned to West Borneo, I was assigned to teach at Immanuel Bible School in Kelansam from 1991 to 1996. Then I was privileged to take graduate studies at Jaffray Theological College in Makassar until 1998. Since returning to West Borneo, I have been teaching at the Theological College in Pontianak.

While studying at Jaffray Theological College my training was enhanced by Mrs. Chapman's patience in training me to catalogue books in the College library. [Natanael was a real encouragement to me when I was given the very difficult assignment of recataloguing the college library books. He was one of the students who said, "I like what you are doing. Can I help you?" He helped me in his after-class hours. –a.c.]

My greatest fulfillment has been to see my students from Immanuel Bible School in Kelansam and from the Theological College in Pontianak remain faithful in ministry for God. May my life be an example to them to continually serve the Lord's guidance.

I felt that my learning skills at Jaffray Theological College were also enhanced by Rev. Chapman's detailed translations, which he taught with sincerity. Mr. Chapman usually presented truth with such intensity that he was always in a sweat—"bathing in sweat" (an Indonesian idiom).

I will never forget Rev. Chapman's testimony when he fell victim to untreatable cancer. "Why should I fall victim to cancer?" Mr. Chapman said. Then added, "Why not me?" The lesson I learned from that was to never complain when God leads us in painful paths.

Sincerely,
Rev. Natanael Semuel, October 15, 1999

* * * * * * *

Rev Simeon Sura, also a second generation pastor, wrote:

I became a Christian in 1957 when Rev. Germann Eddy came for spiritual emphasis meetings to Immanuel Church, in the Belitang district of West Borneo. As a child, when I heard my father preach in a prayer meeting, I remembered saying, "I want to become a preacher." I was so moved by his example of serving God without considering material rewards.

I was prepared for ministry by both missionary and Indonesian teachers, not only from their teaching but also by the example of their lives. I appreciated Rev. Chapman's firm discipline. Even though some students dreaded it, I accepted his wisdom. I came to the conclusion that there were no significant problems that could not be solved if we had faith in God.

However, when I studied at Jaffray Theological College in Makassar, from 1963 to 1965, I faced many hardships. I was far away from home and all the help I had received from my people. When I became sick with hepatitis I was really lonely. Then during the long school vacation I had to work hard at the Goa Paper Factory. In spite of these difficulties I determined to become more faithful in my studies. In those times I often sought the Lord's help in prayer and appreciated the examples and encouragement of my teachers.

When I returned to West Borneo in 1965, I was assigned to a church-planting ministry for one and a half years, in the Tempunak River area near Kelansam. Besides Sunday ministries I taught in a nearby elementary school. I was convinced that this was God's direction, for some of those children later became the founding fathers of the Jerusalem Church in the Selebak and Srikasul villages there.

I will never forget how Mrs. Chapman cared for my wife when she became ill, looking after her till she recovered. While she was recovering I typed Mrs. Chapman's lessons on New Testament Survey. Learning those lessons while my wife's health was improving was a double blessing.

In 1967 I was assigned to teach at Immanuel Bible School in Kelansam. During my nine years at the school I was always involved in team ministries in the long school vacations. We visited many villages where people had never heard the good news of Jesus.

In the 1970 long vacation I had the privilege of working with the missionary widow, Mrs. Elisabeth Jackson, when she was on assignment at Immanuel Bible School for a short time. Together we took the gospel message to the Undau Tribe, a people who had been headhunters.

In the 1973 long vacation, we sailed up the Melawi River following the footsteps of the Chapmans who did pioneer missionary work from 1953 to 1955 up there. Many people still remembered them. During that same long vacation Rev. Simon Enggah and widow, Mrs. L. Sante, went out on an evangelistic trip to the Ketunggau district.

In another year, with the help of MAF and Christians in the Sekadau River area, I and several students went on an evangelistic trip to give the good news of salvation in Jesus to the Kadah Tribe. I praise the Lord for the support of the C&MA and MAF services to make so much Kingdom growth possible in our province.

In 1978 I studied at the Batu Malang Institute in Java for one year. When I came back I served the Belitang district churches again. Then I taught in the Balai Sepuak Bible School for nine years. In 1991 to 1993 I had another opportunity to study at Jaffray Theological College in Makassar. When I returned to West Borneo I was assigned to church work in Pontianak. My elders and I planted churches in Jeruju, Tanjong Hulu, Siantan and Sungai Raya districts in Pontianak. Praise God, all these churches are still growing.

In 1996 I was assigned to be director of the Balai Sepuak Bible School. Three years later we had 94 students at the school. My greatest joy has been to see my students continue to be faithful in ministry. A verse I claim for myself and my students is Philippians 1:6, "being confident of this, that he who began a good work in you will carry it on to completion until the day of Christ Jesus."

Respectfully,
Rev. Simeon Sura and family, mid-1999

* * * * * * *

Rev. Aheng Pieter, another second generation pastor, wrote:

I received the Lord Jesus as my Saviour at a Belitang district youth camp when I was 16 years old. When Jesus came into my life and filled me with His Holy Spirit I was changed. I experienced deep joy and peace and had a positive attitude about my future.

While attending the youth camp the next year I felt God calling me to full-time service. I struggled with that. Finally with the emphasis of Romans 12:1, I surrendered my life to God. "Therefore, I urge you, brothers, in view of God's mercy, to offer your bodies as living sacrifices, holy and pleasing to God—this is your spiritual act of worship."

Then I remembered my father's words, that as his first-born son I was dedicated to God to replace him in ministry. It was a joy to follow my father's example. So in mid-1966 I became a student at Immanuel Bible School in Kelansam, where I enjoyed all my teachers' lectures.

In my second year it seemed that no one encouraged me. In fact, my student friends laughed at me with disdain. So in mid-year I quit and went home. However, I remembered Rev. Chapman's words that we must always be on our guard and never allow personal feelings to rob us of following the Lord. Instead, we should let God use the gifts he gave us to become a positive example for Him. Once again the Holy Spirit used Romans 12:1 to bring me to obedience to my Lord, and I returned to school.

I was married and studied at Immanuel Bible School in Kelansam again. I served my 1974 to 1975 internship in the Tembaga Village in the Sekadau River area. After I finished my final year at Immanuel Bible School I was appointed to the Gilgal church in the Belitang district. When I was assigned to study at Jaffray Theological College in Makassar in 1977 to 1982, I and my family missed our people who were far away in West Borneo.

During those school days my wife always committed our problems to the Lord. But when money didn't come from our sponsors for three months, we were desperate. Finally, when we heard that some money had been sent for us directly to President Anggu at our College, we praised God and were able to carry on.

When we were concerned about our children's education, we were pleased to hear that The Gamaliel Christian School offered free schooling for the children of Jaffray College students. That's when God reminded us how He had also miraculously provided food for us in our first church-planting assignment in West Borneo. Two times we had been without food for three days. The second time, when our two year-old child was crying because he was hungry, we prayed that even without food God would keep him healthy.

At that time a Muslim merchant neighbor came to visit and asked us how we were supported. We answered that we had no promised support. The merchant was amazed, and added that as a newcomer to the province he had also experienced hunger. He then asked his servant to bring us rice, cooking oil, salt fish, eggs, sugar, tea and coffee. We felt like our Lord had sent the ravens to feed us—just like He fed Elijah.

This act of kindness encouraged us to believe that God would establish His church in Tembaga Village, on the Sekadau River. That fellowship of believers did indeed become strong. They even sent us some money while we were studying at Jaffray College.

When we returned to West Borneo I was assigned to teach at my alma mater, Immanuel Bible School in Kelansam. To me it was always a joy to see my students finish well by becoming faithful servants for God. Later, I was assigned to teach in the Balai Sepuak Bible School where I still serve.

We appreciated the Chapmans for their commitment to God, always teaching us the things that are most important for ministry. I especially thank Mrs. Chapman for her concerns for our family while I studied at Jaffray Theological College in Makassar. I will never forget how she taught me three levels of English as a Second Language in a period of time when only two levels were taught.

I will always remember how the Chapman family became special friends of my father, Rev. U. Pieter. Both Rev. Chapman and my father died of cancer. They must be laughing and enjoying each other in heaven.

Lovingly submitted,
Rev. Aheng Pieter, October 15, 1999

* * * * * * *

Rev. Jilim E. wrote:

My parents were Christians and as a child I diligently attended Sunday school. However, as a teenager I rebelled against the Lord and lived in sin. Then at a Passover (Easter) celebration I was impressed by the preaching of Rev. Bua. But it was not the Word of God that challenged me—it was his skillful preaching that interested me. In my heart I wanted to be able to speak like that. That's what prompted me to go to Immanuel Bible School in Kelansam in 1964.

But I did not receive Christ as Saviour until 1965. Gradually I began to follow the ways of God. Even then I was not yet convinced that I should become a servant of God full-time. When I prayed asking God to release me from being His servant, I finally received full assurance that I was indeed doing God's will. I praised God that I was successful in my studies. In 1969 to 1970 I served my one-year internship at the Nanga Lemak Church and returned to finish my studies. I faithfully served the Lord in the churches assigned to me.

I had the privilege of being appointed to take four years of studies at Jaffray Theological College in Makassar. Upon my return to West Borneo, I was assigned to teach at my alma mater, Immanuel Bible School in Kelansam.

One of my responsibilities was to be director of the boys' dormitory. That became a big challenge for me when some of the students lived in rebellion. I finally decided that I would demand good discipline. Some students were dismissed. I praise God that it resulted in changes for the better at our school.

My life motto is: "Once a servant, always a servant, wherever God leads me and for however long He needs me."

Respectfully submitted,
Rev. Jilim E., April 20, 2001

The Chapman family in 1961. Richard and Ken are standing at the back. Seated are Kathleen, Gordon, Adina holding Sylvia, and Tim

CHAPTER 8

LIVING ON THE EDGE

Tomorrow is for people who are willing to live on the edge. A vibrant, paraplegic Christian, who wouldn't allow his disabilities to hinder him said, "If you're not living on the edge, you are taking up too much space." How did that concept affect us as we faced pressures in West Borneo? Without adequate opportunity for emotional and physical recovery times, survival would be very difficult.

We recognized that the difference between excellence and mediocrity would depend on the choices we made. Knowing that God wanted us to be responsible stewards of the gifts of grace He gave us, how would we respond when confronting a dilemma? We could not possibly foresee the implications of our commitment to God. What we did know was that facing complications would test our endurance and stability. Jesus' emphasis was, "… If anyone would come after me, he must deny himself and take up his cross daily and follow me. For whoever wants to save his life will lose it, but whoever loses his life for me will save it." (Luke 9:23-24) In the final analysis, would we be ready when we "tasted" fear?

* * * * * * *

In 1961, while still living in Balai Sepuak, when all the missionaries were leaving for conference in Java, we loaded onto our houseboat our baggage, camping equipment and food for the five-day journey. Students on board were hired as seamen. Waving good-bye to the Indonesians who would watch the campus in our absence, we began our trip. Suddenly the bow of our launch ran aground on the fork of a large, submerged tree. No matter what we tried to do, we could not dislodge the boat. We needed an alternate plan.

After transferring all the necessary baggage to a large outboard motorboat and covering things with tarpaulins in case of rain, we set out on a voyage with many restrictions and

83

inconveniences. This trip was most difficult for our two veterans, Lillian Marsh and Margaret Kemp. After a trip of about 14 hours we finally arrived at the nearest regency town of Sanggau, where we found lodging in the home of a Chinese family. Gordon had to return to Balai Sepuak with the mission outboard and its contents. He eventually arrived at our field conference after us, several days late.

While four of our missionary colleagues cleared important documents at the government office, I quickly set up beds and prepared for a short stay. We also sent a message to a colleague in the port city of Pontianak. He immediately set out by jeep to get us. Though there were too many people for one jeep, we determined to risk the inconveniences so we could all travel in one trip. We arrived in Pontianak exhausted, but were glad to be in our temporary home. However, we still had to get passage on the next available plane to Jakarta, which meant going to the airport repeatedly, always prepared to fly out if seats were provided. In Jakarta our staff arranged for the last four hours of travel by car to the conference site in Bandung.

These kinds of interruptions and delays were not uncommon for missionaries who worked in East and West Borneo at that time. In spite of all these difficulties, conference was always an important renewal time. Together with friends we shared our struggles, joys and victories since our last meeting two years prior. And we also deliberated many plans for the future of each of our stations.

* * * * * * *

In 1964 we faced a significant challenge. Our Bible School had to move to the Kelansam campus between academic terms. With a loaded mission launch it was a 14-hour trip one way between the two sites. Six missionary colleagues, two Indonesian teachers and their families, and six students assisted with this formidable task.

The first and most important reason for the move was to situate the campus more centrally to the National Church districts we served. Land was purchased on the Kapuas, a main river connected to many smaller tributaries. The nearest government regency centre was just 40 minutes upstream from Kelansam by outboard motorboat. Traveling on a main river meant that we would have a more navigable waterway during the dry season. It would also open far-reaching opportunities to make contact with people who had never heard the good news of salvation in Jesus.

Although the project had been ongoing for several years, we weren't fully prepared for it. A contractor had been using our mission launch manned by mission staff to have lumber brought up from Pontianak. To add to the building supplies and pay for their school fees, diligent students at the Balai Sepuak campus prepared lumber with a handsaw. A rubber tree grove and some fruit trees grew on the land. Students cleared portions of the property to make room for the buildings needed. It was a good location. In the meantime personnel transported lumber from Balai Sepuak to Kelansam on weekend trips.

In 1963 when we were preparing to move, a few buildings on the Kelansam campus were already completed, but not nearly enough to house all the people who would be living there. However, at the school board meeting that year it was decided that mid-1964 was the best time to relocate to the new campus because the Alliance missionaries had scheduled their biennial field conference in Bandung, Java to take place in mid-1965. There wouldn't be enough time left for a move during the conference year.

Our local Dyak friends were not happy to see us leave. They had depended on the services of the staff and student body. The Kelansam site was too far away for workers to make weekend trips to the Belitang district churches. It was a huge adjustment for the Dyaks as well as for our whole school family. In later years, to compensate for this, the Indonesian brethren opened another feeder Bible school at Balai Sepuak.

The final graduation at the Ebenezer Church near the Balai Sepuak Bible School was an historic end of an era. Balai Sepuak was the district in which Rev. Arthur Mouw had witnessed the significant move to Christianity before World War II. Just after the war Rev. Schisler opened this first West Borneo Bible school.

The district youth conference, a vital event for the young people of the area, was held on the old campus right after graduation. In June, our colleague, Peter Nanfelt, moved Teacher Simon and his family and some missionaries' personal effects to the Kelansam campus.

The school board decided that we should not cancel a full school year to accomodate the move. But it seemed unreasonable to relocate the school to Kelansam in the middle of the dry season—the longer school vacation. Because of low water levels

Gordon wrote, "Very often a canoe with an outboard motor could not navigate the upper Belitang River, where the old campus was located, much less a large launch fully loaded with supplies. Since this problem was beyond our control, we had to commit it to the Lord and set to work to overcome difficulties that were within our reach."

When two launches were fully loaded and ready for takeoff, Gordon became fearful. Weren't we being irrational? Together we sat down to discuss what looked to be impossible. Because of some rains upstream, we had experienced a flash flood. But Gordon feared the river was not high enough. Since rains rarely came at that time of year, it seemed to me that we might be missing the last chance to get out if we didn't try. In the end we trusted God for miracles. We began the move to Kelansam the first week of July 1964.

Gordon wrote, "By this time the Belitang River had dropped until we couldn't run the two mission launches out. We had to drift out, using ropes and poles, sometimes actually raising the boats out of difficulties. After drifting and poling for several hours we were able to proceed cautiously by using the launches' motors to get to the mouth of the Belitang River." Once we entered the Kapuas River, navigation was much easier.

Likewise, with the added help of missionary colleague Bill Kuhns, Indonesian teacher Bua' and a half dozen students, several more trips were made in the next few weeks. They transported school freight and Indonesian teachers' and missionaries' household items. On the final trip Teacher Bua's family also moved.

Gordon reported, "In all of these trips, during this potentially difficult time of year, we had adequate water to make full use of our two mission launches. On occasion, between trips, the river dropped to impossible levels, but when we needed to travel there was sufficient water to get the boats out. We give all the praise to God. Local people commented on our foolishness to move things out on the Belitang River in the dry season, but when we sailed out with sufficient water for our need, they said we were fortunate. Some recognized that it was of God." Indeed, it was His miraculous provision!

Meanwhile, I faced a dilemma. With the launches arriving in Kelansam with load after load, I was on the receiving end. How could I find space for everything in our two-bedroom home? School supplies in wooden crates were piled high in our small office. Lela Pierce and Helen Hall's household effects were stacked in the second bedroom. A lot of extra things filled our bedroom, a small storeroom and our living room. Each time a load arrived, students helped me pile things higher, while making narrow paths to move around in the house.

When Lela Pierce and Helen Hall arrived back from furlough, the house intended for their home merely had the floor, the girders and a roof constructed. Fortunately, they wanted to visit the old campus one more time. They decided to go back to Balai Sepuak on the last trip before the start of the new school-year's classes. That gave me my window of opportunity. With the help of some school boys, I stacked Lela and Helen's belongings as high as possible in the second bedroom of our home, allowing just enough space for a cot and a table for each of them. The boys also helped me rearrange the study to make all records and class materials accessible for immediate use.

In the meantime, as Gordon wrote, "When we arrived at the mouth of the Belitang River, the Army Post there would not allow us to go upstream, nor were we allowed to return home. We were under house arrest in our own boat." In fact all boats going upstream or downstream were held up at the mouth of the river. Nobody knew if it would be for several days or several weeks. Our folks began to ration their food supply. Thankfully, several days later they were released to proceed. As he was leaving to go downstream, a missionary friend called out to Gordon, "If you ever find out why we were held up, please let me know."

Because of time constraints, Gordon's plan to bring another load of freight from Balai Sepuak had to be cancelled. Only Teacher Bua' and six students with him went on to Balai Sepuak with an outboard motorboat to get a supply of rice for the school year. Gordon, Lela and Helen returned to Kelansam.

Why were they held under house arrest in their own boats? Some time later we heard that rumours had spread of "enemy parachute droppings" in the Belitang district. Government officials from the regency town downstream had come up to investigate. Apparently their search proved unproductive. But general political unrest in the province was increasing. We even observed military manoeuvres in the centre of the regency town of Sintang. We wondered what they were preparing for.

We and our friends and missionary colleagues often had unnerving experiences, especially as we traveled up and down on the main river. At one checkpoint, about ten hammer-and-sickle flags flew high at the river's edge, an imposing sight. Officials came aboard our boats making unrealistic demands. They ordered cups of coffee and turned our radio on. They demanded some of the food they saw, produce which our colleagues upstream had ordered. It wasn't ours to give away, but we were forced to hand it over. Responding diplomatically was always a challenge.

Military personnel frequently demanded free rides on our boats. They fired their guns in the air from the river's edge as a signal for a ride. They had to be picked up right then, a frightening experience that often terrified our students who were our assistants on the boat. On other occasions I panicked when I saw government officials coming up the path to our home on the Bible School campus. Why were they coming? A year later we would understand what these unnerving events meant. It was the beginning of a communist strategy to take over of the whole country of Indonesia.

Students moving the 1,500-watt plant from Balai Sepuak to Kelansam, providing a limited amount of electricity for our students and staff

Meanwhile, preparations continued in high gear for the beginning of classes at our new campus. Teacher Bua' and the young men put up a temporary village-type building for male student housing and added a large area for chapel space. When school finally began, classes had to be held on porches, on covered walkways and in every available space. It was a simple beginning.

At that time, we faced another imminent deadline. In just over two months, four of our children would be coming home from boarding school. Their bedroom spaces in our home were still full of freight. The two missionary ladies were still temporarily housed in that second crowded bedroom. Could the carpenters be encouraged to speed up their work? They were unskilled, bristly, "prison labour" carpenters, performing community service instead of being incarcerated. Before our arrival in Kelansam, these arrangements had been made by an absentee contractor. Teacher Bua' had already experienced problems in settling some of their impulsive intrusions into our students' lives. Also, the carpenters had used the school's lumber to build furniture to sell to neighbours in nearby villages. Despite these difficulties, building continued. Finally, near the end of October, Lela and Helen were able to move into their own unfinished home. And we had time to make space for our children's homecoming in mid-November.

Although most of the buildings the carpenters had put up were not yet completed, some of their construction was already falling down. Rotting boards and girders had been installed in places difficult to reach. Cracked asbestos ceiling sheets were sagging and needed to be replaced. Many structural problems remained unsolved. Eventually we halted construction. When new contractors from a nearby town were employed we had no more major complaints.

With so many distractions, it was difficult to develop a good spiritual atmosphere for our students' study times. But God was there when we needed Him in that first year on our new campus. Working together with our Indonesian and missionary teachers was a joy. And now that we were no longer in a "Christian" area, we needed to build a vision of reaching our new community.

Gordon reported, "There are many opportunities for witness and service. ... 'Lift up your eyes and look on the fields' is our goal. We desire to develop a good practical work program which would help the students use what they are studying in their classes."

In that first year on the new campus, the Belitang district planned to hold their National Church Conference in Balai Sepuak during the first week in December. Gordon was invited to be their devotional speaker. It also gave us an opportunity to pick up school supplies and missionaries' things we had left behind. With so many interruptions, we struggled to develop memorable family Christmas times for our children's annual vacation at home. Years later, after our older children had returned to Canada for college, the Mission made more vacation times available for families.

Looking back and remembering the many demanding transitions for our family, for our teachers and all the students during that first school year at the new campus, we were astounded at how God intervened. It changed forever who we all were. The sacrificial services of the Indonesians and missionaries proved to be invaluable, for they worked together to make possible the new start at the Kelansam campus. No doubt, much suffering was never verbalized.

* * * * * * *

By 1965, menacing clouds framed the horizon. Indonesia faced the 1965 September 30 Movement (G30S). It was an explicit strategy to bring the whole country under communist rule. Beginning in the capital city of Jakarta, wave by wave, every city, town and hamlet was supposed to come under the control of communist leaders. President Sukarno had developed this detailed strategy with the help of communist rulers in China.

To put the whole country under suppression, specific provisions were made available in every government centre throughout the nation. Lists of people's names that would not approve of Communism were available in each office, along with torture instruments for the cruel measures of their elimination. Missionaries, church leaders, government workers and all adults who could not or would not submit to communist rule would be killed. Children would be saved for indoctrination. We found out after the fact that a mass grave had been made ready for us near our regency town of Sintang.

But God had other plans. Our Lord is a master at controlling crises. The 30th of September Movement coup d'etat was immediately followed on October 1st by a counter-coup. The Indonesian military, a large resisting force, fought against the coup. On the evening of the revolutionary event, six of the military's top generals became victims of the struggle. Others were spared by divine intervention. The generals who had been killed were thrown into a dry well (crocodile hole). Today, just outside the city of Jakarta, a memorial park called Lobang Buaya (Crocodile Hole) tells the story. Life-sized statues of the generals stand on a high wall above a massive etched mural, immortalizing for all to see the bloody history of communism in Indonesia. For days after the resistance, bodies of hundreds of victims, especially in Java, floated down the rivers. Impaled heads perched on fence posts. It was reported that some killings may have been out of revenge.

Remembering the details of those gruesome events still leaves me stunned. When we later visited Lobang Buaya, it brought home to us the full force of the power of God in delivering the country from a massive blood bath. Fortunately, where we lived in upcountry West Borneo, there were few victims.

Details about the struggle were mind-boggling! We later heard about our friend Pastor Idrus in the Kayan district, in the interior of West Borneo, who felt compelled to call his church to fast and pray for a day, for a second day and again for a third day for a crisis in their country. Though they were totally unaware of the details, God had called them to fast and pray till the military had regained control. The complexities of secretly getting rid of torture instruments were reported. The churches and Christians realized that God had given them another chance.

Even more amazing were the daily trials held in Jakarta after the coup, for a period of many months. The trials, aired throughout the country over short-wave radio, were for the President's first aide. By trying the aide, the President was also implicated. However, since the poor people in Java revered him, he was not in much danger. He lived under house arrest in a comfortable home until his death.

Why did God allow these horrific things to happen in Indonesia? That's a hard question to answer. It certainly was a serious wake-up call in October 1965 for all the Christians. But as a recent news commentator said, the events of those days pale in comparison to what is happening in Indonesia in the 21st century. The increase in natural disasters and the escalating, worldwide conflicts between ethnic groups, with the exacerbation of persecution and harassment of Christians, far exceeds anything that has ever happened. What can we say? Is God preparing us for the end times as described in Matthew 24:21, "For there will be a great distress, unequalled from the beginning of the world until now—and never to be equalled again." World-wide, the increase of wickedness, brutality and revenge, the lack of compassion and the villainous behaviour of man against man is shocking. But we have a just God. "For he has set a day when He will judge the world with justice by the man he has appointed. He has given proof of this to all men by raising him from the dead." (Acts 17:31)

One thing is sure—never before have so many people been open to hear about Jesus, the Saviour of the world. In the midst of terrible persecution and devastation, more than at any other time in history, people are seeking God. And Christians who persevere become more fervent through suffering, producing "… a harvest of righteousness and peace for those who have been trained by it." (Hebrews 12:11) This is God's plan for greater victory. He is preparing people, especially Christians, for His final return at the end of the age as described in Matthew 24.

* * * * * * *

In June 1967, Gordon and I needed to attend two simultaneous graduations. Our son Ken was graduating from high school in Malaysia, while Gordon was appointed to looking after the graduation at our Immanuel Bible School. And although I had done a lot of the packing ahead of time, he would have to do the final packing and preparation for our furlough. During this period, each of us faced our own crisis.

Missionary colleague John Van Patter took me and my five year-old daughter, Sylvia, to Pontianak by mission launch. On arriving at our rented house in Pontianak we found that someone had broken into it. They had ransacked the cupboards throughout the house. Some of our family's personal effects were stolen, including suitcases with Sylvia's and my good travel clothes. The first evening there, I sat at the kitchen table, completing the Bible School's bookkeeping so that John could take the records and the extra cash for the school upstream the next day. Furthermore, John had given me enough cash to buy all our missionaries' airfares from Pontianak to Jakarta. Our colleagues would all be coming down to Pontianak, hoping to get early flights to Java for the field conference.

Once again, while Sylvia and I were alone in bed, a thief tried to break into our house. The intruder disconnected our electricity. Coming back time after time to test the closed shutters, he gave me no rest all night. By then I had locked our bedroom door from the inside. I decided that if I heard him trying to break in I would immediately cry out for help to a very kind neighbour, whose bedroom window was opposite mine. When I heard his crashing noises in the back kitchen, I opened my window and frantically called out for help. The thief escaped, leaving bloody stains behind in the back rooms.

The next morning I took Sylvia with me to the airline ticket office to get rid of the cash in my hands. When we came back to the house I quickly packed our bags and got a pedicab to take us to the home of missionary friends who lived in the city. Just as I was leaving, a young man wearing dark glasses appeared right at my elbow, asking me where I was going. Terrified, because of his proximity, I shook like a leaf. I assured him I would be back. But I had no intention of coming back to sleep in that dangerous environment. I would merely come back in the daytime to check if the electricity had been reconnected as I had requested. In time Sylvia and I caught a flight to Jakarta, where Sylvia stayed with missionary friends while I attended Ken's graduation in Tanah Rata, Malaysia. After graduation Ken and Richard joined me on a flight back to Jakarta, where I picked up Sylvia. After a four-hour drive up the mountain, we finally reconnected with the rest of our family in Bandung, the conference location.

During my crisis in Pontianak, Gordon's crisis in Kelansam was secretly brewing. It was preceded by the blessings of Rev. Kamasi's preaching. He had come from Jaffray Theological College in Makassar to be the graduation speaker in Kelansam. His practical, straightforward presentation of the Word of God deeply impressed our students, many of whom made advances in their spiritual lives. Immediately after the graduation, the National Church held a pastors' conference. Once again, Rev. Kamasi blessed his audience with his excellent preaching ministry.

At that time the Kelansam Bible School sent a letter to the National Church Pastors' Conference requesting that Simeon Surah, a recent graduate of the Jaffray Theological College in Makassar, be added to our teaching staff. Simeon, the conference secretary, typed the minutes and Gordon took time to duplicate them for the delegates.

Later, Simeon brought another brief report to Gordon, which in one detail was contrary to an original conference decision. In that point, a few of the older Indonesian leaders were rejecting us as returning missionaries. It was a total surprise. We had not heard of any dissension, nor did we have a voice in the ultimate decision. Simeon apologized, saying that most of the delegates were not in favour of what had happened, giving details of the background. The Indonesian leaders with whom we worked felt betrayed, saying, "If the elders rejected the Chapmans, what missionaries would they accept?" Gordon was numb with shock, but his response was to leave the problem with God. One author wrote, "Let criticism and hurts become the building blocks in the next step of your journey." We received their unilateral decision, knowing that God would bring the best out of it.

Some months later our mission conference decided that a one-sided decision was invalid. Both parties must be given a fair hearing before any action would be taken. Years later, in the 1980s, the Indonesian brethren proved their warm appreciation of our services by calling us back to West Borneo for several, very enjoyable ministry opportunities.

Looking back now, we know that God had a far-reaching agenda for us. In spite of delicate issues, walking away from obedience to God was never an option. In the end we would be working with the National Church on different islands, learning to understand their people and preparing many dear servants for the Kingdom during the most fruitful years ahead. For the present, our challenge remained: intense prayer and waiting on God. How did we conquer all our fears during those difficult days? God gave us the courage to trust Him again and again, one crisis at a time. Several verses from a favourite hymn were so appropriate:

Not I but Christ be honoured, loved, exalted;
Not I but Christ be seen, be known, be heard;
Not I but Christ in every look and action;
Not I but Christ in every thought and word.

Christ, only Christ, no idle word e're falling;
Christ, only Christ, no needless bustling sound;
Christ, only Christ, no self-important bearing;
Christ, only Christ, no trace of 'I' be found.

Refrain:

Oh, to be saved from myself, dear Lord! Oh to be lost in Thee!
Oh, that it might be no more I, but Christ that lives in me!

—Albert B. Simpson

The Chapman family, in 1967, holding Indonesian artifacts.
Sylvia, Adina and Tim (front row)
Kathleen, Ken, Gordon and Richard (back row)

CHAPTER 9

<u>FAMILY PRIORITIES</u>

The Psalmist said, "Children are an heritage from the Lord." (Psalm 127:3b KJV) In fact, they are the most valuable heritage. They are flesh and blood of their parents, with an individuality derived from the genetics of generations of their ancestors. And God wanted to bless the family unit in succeeding generations so He charged parents to pass on His divine plan for His people to the end of time, "These commandments that I give you today are to be upon your hearts. Impress them on your children. Talk about them when you sit at home and when you walk along the road, when you lie down and when you get up." (Deuteronomy 6:6-7)

The missionary family unit in its adopted country holds a unique function. It corporately presents a system of Christian family values to the local people; and for the parents and their children it creates a wholeness of fellowship and comfort in a country where they are far away from their homeland and extended families. Because children are loved the world over, an added blessing is that they often open doors of communication with members of another culture like nothing else can.

MKs' (missionary kids') experiences abroad are no more all positive than they are for their peers in their home country. In today's fractured world children can feel neglected in any country. However, in their adventures of growing up in a foreign country our children experienced things North American children could hardly imagine.

* * * * * * *

It was time to return to Indonesia. Our year's home leave had ended. We departed from Victoria in mid-1962 with the usual good-byes. But upon arrival in Frankfurt, Germany we faced a startling situation. Unprecedented emergencies affecting Rich and Ken's travels to get to school in Vietnam seemed almost unsolvable. We had flown to Canada over the Pacific in mid-1961 and were returning to the Far East over the Atlantic just under a year later, taking a more economical round-the-world flight scheduled by our mission.

In the Frankfurt airport, the KLM desk clerk declared, "You have troubles!" The airline had cancelled all flights to Saigon because Vietnam had been declared a war zone. KLM had not informed us of this cancellation. We had confirmed tickets to take Rich, aged 12 and Ken, aged 13, to Saigon and then upcountry to Dalat to get them settled at the Alliance boarding school. For them, it was a new school in a new country. The desk clerk called the KLM station manager. A lengthy investigation and much discussion followed. Their only alternative was to fly us to Singapore, and from there we would have to arrange for a flight to Saigon on another airline.

In Singapore, after days of difficult negotiations with various airlines, Pan American Airlines provided tickets for the boys without extra airfares. But with the time-consuming delays, our own exit/re-entry visas for Indonesia were running out. How could we possibly send our young boys unaccompanied on an unfamiliar journey to Saigon and then on to Dalat? Our only recourse was to send a telegram to Mr. Dutton, the Alliance business agent in Saigon, to meet them. The Pan Am representative in Singapore responded, "Your telegram might not get there." Instead, they offered to telex their Saigon agent, sending him Mr. Dutton's phone number and address. Our son, Ken tells the story:

> On the day of our flight we put on our good travel clothes. Our parents explained how we would arrive in Saigon, another country. We'd go through customs and immigration. There, a tall white man with white hair would meet us. Mother even wrote out his name and phone number and pinned it inside my jacket pocket. They prayed with us, and Dad put us on the plane. It was a scary adventure to walk on alone. We waved goodbye from the plane. We filled out declaration papers. I declared my clarinet, and Rich declared his trumpet, and we set out to enjoy our flight.
>
> When we got to Saigon we went through immigration. Then we picked up our bags and went through customs. Nobody was there to meet us. We spent an hour searching the airport for Mr. Dutton. We prayed and wondered what to do. Then an army officer approached us who spoke broken English. He asked, "Where are you going?" I showed him the address and telephone number for Mr. Dutton. He took me

into his office, and I phoned Mr. Dutton, while Rich watched our bags. Mr. Dutton came and took us to his house [the Mission guest house in Saigon].

Mr. Dutton made reservations for our plane trip to Dalat the next morning. He thought a grade ten girl would be on that flight. But when we got to the airport, the plane had left an hour earlier. So the following day we took a plane to Dalat. When we arrived, nobody was there to meet us. The Duttons had given us the phone number for Dalat School. Richard said, "It's my turn!" He asked a storekeeper for a phone and called the school. Mrs. Fitzstevens answered the phone and said that her husband was on his way to the airport and would pick us up.

Mrs. Fitzstevens, at the school, picks up the story:

Dear Mrs. Chapman,

Your boys arrived in good shape and seem to be happy in their new surroundings. We're sorry you couldn't get up here with them as it is so much nicer to picture them in their new environment.

They probably told you about the mix-up in Saigon. We didn't have word of their arrival either. They called from the airport, which is quite a distance out of town. Since we were expecting the missionary children from Thailand when they phoned, my husband was on his way to the airport, but he didn't know that your boys were there. He saw these two white boys in the lounge and asked them if they had a ride. They said, "Yes." When the Thai plane came in, no children were on it. He saw the two boys still sitting there and asked them again who the man was that was meeting them? They said, "Mr. Fitzstevens." He answered, "I'm Mr. Fitzstevens!" So they finally made it.

We didn't hear about these travel delays until some weeks later. By that time we had to be back in the interior of West Borneo where we had no quick way of communicating. Thankfully, our boys had become adept world travelers.

At Christmastime Ken and Rich traveled from Dalat to Saigon, changed planes and flew to Singapore, where once again they changed planes to get to Jakarta. There our Mission guest house staff picked them up and put them on the first available commercial flight to Pontianak. One of us, traveling with our

Borneo colleagues, was on hand to receive them to bring them upriver to our station, another five-day trip by our mission's houseboat. Traveling in a foreign country in the sixties as young boys, their whole trip was a long, risky journey. In later years, an adult usually accompanied our children from Jakarta to their school abroad.

* * * * * * *

In 1965, Dalat School was forced to relocate to Bangkok, Thailand. For some time the escalating guerilla warfare in Vietnam had caused deep concern for the parents of the missionary children. They urged our Mission directors to move the school to a safer place. Parents were also asked to find an alternate place for the children's schooling in their home countries in case a location for the boarding school could not be found in the Far East. We made tentative arrangements for Ken and Rich to go to Victoria, Canada, to stay with Chuck and Eily Chapman. If that happened, we would not see our boys for several years. Thankfully, a place was found in Bangkok. The U.S. Air Force offered to evacuate them, but for security reasons the evacuation had to be done on short notice.

On Saturday morning, April 15, the Dalat School bell rang. Bells didn't ever ring on Saturday! The students hurried to the Assembly Hall. They were told that Easter Monday, April 17, would be moving day. The U.S. Embassy in Saigon reported that they could no longer guarantee their safety in Dalat. The school would have 48 hours to pack up everything. The students were promised that they'd keep their "Dalat School" name. And yes, they'd take their ice-cream machine. Older students did their own packing and were also assigned to assist younger students to pack up their belongings. Easter Sunday morning the choir sang their cantata at sunrise as planned. Then they changed into work clothes and hastened to finish their packing.

Early Monday morning military transport buses arrived to drive everyone to the airport. Ken and three of his buddies were assigned to stay behind to check the campus in detail. They had to make sure that nothing important was left behind. Then, by jeep, an air force driver took them to the airport. Three C-123 transport planes were being loaded to evacuate the children, the staff and all necessary school supplies in one flight.

As they flew south along the Cambodian border, suddenly three Communist jets, with firing capability, came alongside to make sure that the U.S. C-123s didn't enter Cambodian territory. It was a very tense moment for the American crews who were unarmed. The enemy planes were so close that the younger children, blissfully unaware of the dangerous situation, waved at the pilots they saw sitting in the cockpits.

Upon arrival at the Saigon airport the C-123s were refueled. All the children had to disembark, but they were not allowed to go to the transit lounge. While standing on the tarmac, in the tropical midday sun, the Alliance guest house staff from Saigon kindly served them sandwiches and cold drinks before they continued their flight. Back in West Borneo, we heard of their evacuation on short-wave radio FEBC from Manila.

The American school children had special immigration status in Thailand, but Ken and Richard were Canadians. Every few months they were required to travel out of country to get their visas renewed. The mission business agent found it most convenient to send them by train from Bangkok to Chiang Mai, a border town in northern Thailand. There they would cross the river to Vientiane, Laos, where our missionaries provided accommodation for them in the guest house. During one holiday period, Gordon and I took Sylvia and specifically traveled to Bangkok to visit our boys. To our dismay they had been delayed in Vientiane. We took the train up there to find out why.

Sylvia, Ken and Richard wait at the front of a C-123 Troop Transport in Vientiane, Laos

Visiting the embassies in Vientiane, Gordon discovered that the boys would never be issued visas under their circumstances.

He was speechless. And there was no way they could return to Bangkok unless they had tickets to leave the country within 24 hours. We had Ken and Richard brought to Jakarta where Gordon received new passports for them. He immediately requested landed immigrant visas for Thailand for our kids. That seemed to be the fastest, most feasible way to get them back to school in Bangkok.

But time was limited. If their visas weren't granted by the first of September, they had to be flown home to Victoria, Canada, to stay with their Uncle Chuck and Aunt Eily Chapman to finish high school. Thank God, on the deadline date, word came that their visas were being issued. When our boys arrived back at Dalat School in Bangkok, they were seven weeks late—a challenge for them at the high school level. But we were grateful that they would be home for Christmas, and that they'd be with us in the Far East until our next furlough. It took a big load off of our minds.

* * * * * * *

Another move for Dalat School was inevitable. "It was the worst of times," is how teacher Ruth Kelck described their eight-month stay in Bangkok at the American Club. Not meant to be a school, the location was far from ideal. Miss Kelck further reported, "Triple-decker beds made it possible to put eight or nine students in one room. That was bearable until the electricity went off and the fans weren't functioning. And it never did work for 50 boys to have three bathrooms. The teachers and students often faced flooded classrooms, where children were more interested in catching frogs than doing school work." With the campus flooded in the rainy season, there was no place for sports activities. Finally the administration found a better location. In January of 1966, school began in the cool climate of the Cameron Highlands in Tanah Rata, Malaysia.

It was a delightful change for the students. The new facility at the Eastern Hotel featured a sizable campus with various kinds of sports activities to enjoy. But small-town Tanah Rata also had limitations. Staff and their families lived in several hotel rooms, and they all had to eat in the catered dining room. Classes were held in hallways and in tin-roofed Quonset huts—a very difficult situation when it poured rain. Gradually, small chalets were built for classrooms and family housing.

The multiple benefits in this new setting were so liberating for the students. There was freedom to roam the jungle trails, catch butterflies, swim at the waterfalls and have cookouts and picnics. Intramural sports activities boosted the morale of high school students. Especially exciting was the fury of a tiger scare when the man-eater was shot near the town. The children were invited to see it. On another occasion the senior boys had the adventure of joining the search team to look for Jim Thompson, Thailand's silk magnate, who was thought to have disappeared in the woods nearby. Jim's disappearance made the world news. He was never found.

Ken, in Kalimantan, looking through the skeleton of a decayed leaf

A Maori barbecue, put on by the Kiwi Regiment from New Zealand for all the students and staff, was a classic. They roasted a whole pig in an eight-foot deep pit, Kiwi-style. Red-hot rocks were positioned in the bottom of the pit on which they layered banana leaves. Next they placed the vegetables and meat, followed by more banana leaves. After topping the pit with soil, hot water was added, which seeped down to the hot rocks, steaming the food over several hours. The barbecue fed the whole regiment, the staff and the students. The regiment played a game of basketball against the school team and also played a game of soccer, mixing their team with the school's to create fair competition.

And when the U.S. President, Lyndon B. Johnson, came to Kuala Lumpur for a visit, their Embassy invited the entire school to be on hand to see him. Everybody was treated to A&W

103

hamburgers and milkshakes. These were some of the more memorable times.

The highlands were wonderful, but there were drawbacks. The British military withdrew from Tanah Rata. With that, Dalat School lost the advantage of medical facilities nearby. As an answer to prayer, a rest and recreation centre which the British military had used became available in Penang. On April 19, 1971, six years to the day after Dalat School had moved from Dalat, Vietnam, the director and business manager negotiated a lease in Sandycroft, Penang, Malaysia. Thirty years later they are still there in spite of notable demands for this valuable, oceanfront property.

* * * * * * *

A shocking news flash on our short-wave radio in West Borneo distressed Gordon. The FEBC gave a brief, muffled and vague report telling of the murder of an American woman by the name of Pat Groff. Could it be that they were talking about our new school teacher in Bandung? Kathy and Tim were in the Alliance elementary school there. Surely we would get direct news from our chairman if it was Pat Groff.

In the confusion of dealing with Pat's horrific death, a belated telegram arrived in Sintang, West Borneo, on March 18. It stated that Patricia Groff was killed by repeated stabbing at 1:50 in the morning on March 6, 1967, just two months after her arrival in Indonesia. Finally, an airmail letter from the school's dorm parents arrived reporting the gory details, a month to the day after the murder. It also reported the empathetic cooperation of the Indonesian government leaders in Bandung and the American Embassy in Jakarta in dealing with the remains.

The morning after Pat's death, other missionaries immediately stepped in to keep classes going in order to maintain a calm transition for the children. Later, the kids were able to study with The American Home Study Group in Bandung. For the beginning of the next school year, Alex Valley from Thunder Bay, Ontario, Canada, came to be their new teacher. But for Kathy and Tim and their fellow students, Pat Groff's death was unforgettable.

* * * * * * *

In the jungles of West Borneo, our children always had a memorable 2-month holiday over Christmas. When he was an older teen, Ken enjoyed the times his Dad allowed him to steer the houseboat on their five-day trip upstream. It gave him a special sense of responsibility. In the heat of the day, the children played games on their bunks or read their favourite books. Richard recalled the sight of thousands of fruit bats passing overhead at dusk, some so low that you could see their incredible wingspan. When Dad turned off the boat's motors to tie up for the night, the nocturnal chatter of the jungle symphony took over. Ken's delight was lying on the roof of the boat to view the stars and to listen to the nightlife. These trips were always a pleasant family cruise.

Tied up to the rain barrel, our beloved Mickey delicately grooms Richard

Although the kids all enjoyed exploring the jungle they were always watchful and leery of snakes. The very colourful small poisonous snakes, the python and the black cobra presented the most danger.

The older kids enjoyed peacefully paddling on the river as they listened to forest life. One day Ken took some of his siblings on a canoe trip up a small creek running beside our house, a cool ride in the heat of the day beneath the lush overhanging jungle growth. Suddenly, the trip was interrupted when Ken had to return home to have me clean and dress the lacerations on his back. He'd sworn his siblings to secrecy. Years later, when they were adults, the truth came out. Their canoe had hit the cord of a monkey trap overhead causing the trap's gate to come crashing down on his back. Fortunately it hadn't hit his head.

One of our children's favourite pets was a little monkey called Mickey. He had been captured in infancy and never grew very big. When they took him for a walk he would cling to their arm and woof-woof at people they passed on the trail. In fun they played various tricks on the "poor beastie" but also gave it special treats, some of which were little house lizards they had caught or leftover food taken from the table. One evening I tried to catch Mickey who had climbed up a tree at dusk. He didn't want to be caught. So I said, "Okay for you, Mickey, you can sleep in the jungle tonight." I started the light generator so that we would have electricity for the evening and went back into the house. There, in the living room, was Mickey! Sneaky monkey!

Tim explained how he caught Mickey by surprise one day. During the midday siesta, Tim snuck out to find Mickey on the ground, with a half-grown chick sitting quietly in his lap. Mickey was grooming the chick's feathers. Mickey—socializing with a chick? Tim left to collect his siblings, who tiptoed out to look over the rail. Suddenly Mickey realized he was being watched. Startled, he punted the chick away with his hind feet, making it fly across the yard. Embarrassed, he scrambled up into his house and hung his head. It was so much like human behaviour that it made the children laugh hilariously, which only aggravated Mickey even more.

Friends asked us to look after a large gibbon ape while they were away. He was a jealous creature that we kept tethered to a pole outside the screened window of the children's bedroom. When he saw me hugging the children he would screech loudly, once even biting one of them when he was within reach. So we shortened his tether. But in the evening, when he was briefly taken off his leash and given some attention, he loved tussling with the younger children in the yard.

A pet for Tim in Sumba was a baby civet cat. It loved to nuzzle in the kids' hair. He also liked to play peek-a-boo around the pillows on Tim's bed. It climbed trees with the children, playfully jumping from branch to branch, just escaping their reach. But as an adult, the civet cat didn't make a good pet because, like a skunk, he would emit an odious protection against his predators.

In West Borneo the children enjoyed ducklings, once observing a "serati" duck softly calling to her hatching ducklings all night long. In the morning they were ready to follow her anywhere. Ken liked watching a mother hen caring for her chicks. He observed the pecking order of chickens, roosters vying for supremacy and chickens conforming to their roosting habits at dusk.

The children usually had cats and dogs for pets. One day they saw a cat jumping to catch something that had dropped out of the rafters. But it pounced back with a great leap because what had fallen was a scorpion. Tim's main interest was very evident so I wrote:

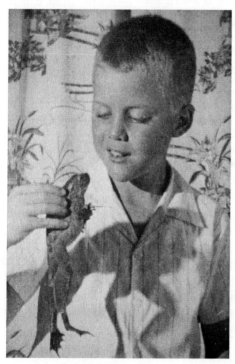

Tim, fascinated by jungle creatures

*Remember your antics
in the jungle, Tim?
You will probably
never forget
the dead python you
dragged around in the
yard
to scare Aunties Helen
and Lela next door.
And the black cobra,
now harmless and
dead in a bucket,
you carried him off
and he couldn't be
found.
When a smell most
offensive and odious
appeared,
the bucket was found
in the pineapple patch.*

*And your scorpion
story, my boy? You cut
off his tail!
With poison sack gone, what harm could he do to anyone?
Hadn't you seen your Dad do the same?
Clever kid you were at five!*

All our children learned to swim. Swimming in the river in the late afternoon, diving and playing tag underwater, having mud-ball fights, and sliding into the river on a mud slide which they shaped on the steep bank—were a few of the many water games. The play-time always ended with a clean bath in the river.

By reading to them in the evenings, Gordon created in each of our children a love for books. Even Sylvia, as a preschooler, loved C.S. Lewis' books. Consequently, as adults their reading habits have been passed on to their own offspring. In Borneo, Gordon took an evening now and then in his photo lab to develop negatives and process photographs. Kathleen and Sylvia cherish the hours they spent watching him work in his darkroom.

Tim was intrigued by the many jungle insects like katydids, praying mantis and centipedes. The large variety of beautiful butterflies and moths captured a lot of interest. Of course he was cautious around wasps, bees, spiders, scorpions, fuzzy caterpillars and their like, since they gave poisonous stings.

Richard remembers wonderful times of solitude, resting in the fork of a wild olive tree near our home. Its pencil-thin vines had climbed a tree, eventually multiplying and becoming so numerous and so big that they killed the host tree. What remained of the core of the original tree was a cave-like sanctuary for numerous iguanas. The top of it formed a platform. There, Richard enjoyed the view of the jungle canopy for hours, not even being frightened when a troop of gibbon apes swung whooping by.

The jungle produces varieties of delicious edible fruits in season. Of the cultivated fruits, some of Ken's favorites were mangos and papayas. Our children all liked citrus fruits such as mandarin oranges and pomelo. Limes made a delicious drink. Soursop was a tasty white fruit that could be eaten as is. Its strained white pulp also made a delicious drink. Or, by adding sweetened condensed milk and then freezing it, it became a tasty sherbet. Indonesia grows about 30 varieties of bananas, the year-round fruit of choice. Mangosteens, rambutan, pineapple, jackfruit and durian were also very popular. So much good health came from eating tropical fruits.

The array of flowers and blooming shrubs in the tropics can easily make the country look like the garden of God. Numerous varieties of orchids thrive in their natural jungle habitat, clinging by their roots to the branches of trees. Collectors around the world pay high prices for these beautiful flowers. In Borneo, the moon-flower vine reached up along the outside of our house, displaying its large white flowers only at night, emitting a heady fragrance.

At Christmas, a special thing for Ken was the homemade plum pudding served with tart lime sauce. Sylvia enjoyed the baking of Christmas treats. The traditional lighting of candles, perched on the boughs of homemade Christmas trees in the church, while *Silent Night* was sung captivated her young heart. During their extended Christmas holidays, Tim, Kathleen and Sylvia played family games and spent fun times at Dr. Jaffray's mountain retreat at Benteng Tinggi, near Makassar, Sulawesi. There the view of the terraced rice paddies, the lush forest growth and the clouds that descended upon us in that cool, mountainous region created a peaceful getaway.

* * * * * * *

In her elementary grades at the Bandung Boarding School, Sylvia enjoyed times of solitude. She loved to stare out of the classroom windows on early mornings smelling the fragrant flowers and watching the sun dance on the glistening dewdrops. She remembers a special camping trip to the mountain town of Lembang. After a hike they spread out their bedrolls and slept under the stars. In the morning they made their own breakfast over a wood fire. First they made a hole in a slice of bread, then put it into a pan on the fire, and cracked an egg into it. Voila!— breakfast! Back at school, she often befriended lonely girls, creating activities just for them.

Grade seven took Sylvia to Dalat School in Penang, Malaysia. Being thrust into a new country and a new circle of friends, she found middle school to be a time of identity-searching. Viewing the sunrise and sunset, hearing the ocean waves and the sounds of rainfall were so comforting. As a young teen she wrote:

The Promise

The sky is pink and opalescent as the sun sinks in its fullness.
After a day's work the sea, green and grey, rests in silence.

I hear the Lord speaking to me,
wooing to melt my heart with the sight,
asking me to revel at the peaceful scene,
to listen to the silence of His presence.

The sun sinks behind the hills,
leaving me in the chill of darkening hours.
The glow of nightfall lingers on my mind, while Christ says to me,
"My child, I will never leave thee nor forsake thee."

During this lonely time Kathleen gave her the book, *Come Away, My Beloved*, by Frances J. Roberts. It had a profound effect on her vision of God. She longed to be and do so many good things that, at 12 years of age, seemed beyond her reach.

In high school some of Sylvia's favourite activities involved choir and octet practices and performances, with concert trips as far away as Kuala Lumpur, a four-hour drive from the school. Other highlights were weekend activities planned by the school staff and cheering on sporting events played by the Dalat Eagles.

For Ken, some highlights at elementary school in Bandung were the weekend hikes. They explored the area for miles. Once they found an abandoned cave used by the armed forces during World War II. Inside they unearthed an old helmet and some bullet casings. Later, when he was in Dalat, Vietnam, they hiked to an abandoned plantation, complete with a stone tower, a big old house with steel barred gates and a swimming pool. It was a place to fantasize about spies, warriors and knights of old.

In Indonesia, Ken enjoyed the drive from Jakarta to Bandung, especially the stop at Puncak Pass (the summit), where it was customary to enjoy treats of large shrimp chips, fried rice and chicken satay. The view of tea plantations in the mountains looked like miles and miles of planted gardens. Pickers with their large conical hats laboured all day collecting the choicest leaves. At dusk large trucks carried the sacks of tea leaves to factories for drying and packaging. During one of their Bandung School weekend outings, the children visited a tea factory to observe the process.

Who were the staff our children most remembered? Richard appreciated Ralph Bressler whose interest in his students fostered learning experiences. Ralph Duell skillfully enhanced his studies in arts and literature. Ken found Mr. Bressler very friendly and fair as a teacher, and he valued him for the way he organized sports. After he started University, Ken sent a letter to Stan Lemon in appreciation for his wisdom and kindness as a dormitory parent. In her senior year Kathleen was so affirmed and blessed by Bob and Bobby Reed when they were her dormitory parents.

Kathleen had a unique experience in 1972, when Queen Elizabeth and Prince Philip paid a royal visit to Penang. Their motorcade was scheduled to drive by the school, but they hadn't made a commitment to stop. However, Ralph Bressler arranged for a special gift for the Queen—a large, gorgeous bouquet of orchids. Kathleen, as a Canadian grade 12 student, had the honor of giving the flowers to the Queen. David Hunt carried the Canadian flag and an American senior student carried the American flag. When the Royal motorcade came by, it did stop. Prince Philip's window opened, and Kathleen presented him with the flowers. The Prince asked her about the school, its children and their parents. She answered, saying that most of the students were children of missionaries who worked in different countries in the Far East.

Kathleen, waiting to present flowers to
Queen Elizabeth II

In Sylvia's senior year, her final trip to Dalat School in Penang turned into quite an adventure. Some of the MKs from various countries in the Far East met in Singapore, planning to travel together to Penang. Upon arrival in Singapore they discovered that the connecting Malaysian Airlines was on strike. This time the MKs had no guardians accompanying them. Via phone connections with the staff at Dalat School and field directors from their various countries of origin, the MKs were booked into a hotel until a reputable bus service was made available to drive them to Penang. How the senior boys so capably handled the situation was amazing. Not only were they responsible for communication connections, they also sweet-talked the immigration officers at the Singapore/Malaysia border to do simplified checks of all the students' baggage!

Their bus arrived at Dalat School after classes had begun. When they drove onto the school campus, friends greeted each other and the travelers shared how they had courageously solved their problems. Sylvia expressed her elation, saying, "At last I have had some travel excitement!" Later, our friend, Dr. Burl

Yarberry, viewed the special affinity MKs hold for one another when he observed them at a stateside reunion. He had never seen anything like it. Their bonding was palpable. Kids were hugging each other and sharing experiences that only their friends could understand.

For all Dalat School seniors, the most memorable time was a secret getaway weekend with their classmates and class sponsors at the end of the year. To sneak away unannounced was part of the excitement! When they returned, the junior class prepared a special meal for them. And every day of their final week, seniors attended memorable events, ending in the baccalaureate service and commencement. No senior ever wanted to miss these celebrations!

After being a staff member at Dalat School for 40 years, Miss Kelck summarized so eloquently the real value of a Christian boarding school experience abroad. She wrote, "Our students still think the most important part of school is their friends and social life; the parents still think Dalat is a safe place providing a quality education; and we teachers still think that our students are the greatest and the best." Most of the students would agree. But the quiet ones often missed the daily environment of home and immediate family. Recently, the Alliance has provided counseling at school and special re-entry seminars for seniors preparing for the inevitable cultural changes upon returning to their home country.

* * * * * * *

Thousands of people worldwide pay dearly for international travel experiences. But for our children it was a fringe benefit, since we had to travel home to Canada once every four years, and a year later return to the Far East. Gordon planned trips to give the family the benefits of seeing many countries in the world.

Some of Ken's travel highlights included eating at the Chinese restaurant in Pontianak, with the sweetened iced tea, buying fresh bread, baked in a large clay oven, from a nearby bakery and helping his Dad buy drums of fuel to take upriver in West Borneo. Ken's impression of the drive along the highway to Agra, India, was seeing so many people, so many animals and so many dusty roads. [To my eyes, seeing the frequent carcasses along the roadside, with great flocks of vultures around them, was more than a cultural education.] Visiting the catacombs in Italy was a great experience for the children. And on one memorable international flight, while crossing the Pacific on a Ticonderoga four-propeller plane, Ken remembered being allowed to go into the cockpit where he had the chance to fly the plane, turning it gently from side to side.

Richard spoke of the independence he felt on a Pan-American Airlines flight from Jakarta to Saigon, with only MKs on board. "We had all the food we wanted—mainly desserts; all the pop we could drink; and a chance to sit at the controls in the cockpit, actually maneuvering the jet, under the control of the pilot of course." Once, while flying with the family, we stopped in India. Richard said, "On arriving at the terminal, when Dad asked me for my passport, I remembered I'd left it in the seat pocket on the plane. Without explanation I ran out, back to the tarmac, hitched a ride on a jeep to the parked plane where the cleaning crew was starting their work. Thankfully it was still where I'd left it. Without too much trouble I was able to hitch a ride back to the terminal. Dad was grim!"

Tim remembers the changing of the guard at Buckingham Palace. [In fact, he was still a small boy at the time. People standing about ten-deep to watch the event was not to his liking. He crawled forward and sat down in front of everyone. We were alarmed when he disappeared in the crowd. But he knew where he was! When the crowd dispersed we found him.] Tim relates other adventures like sitting in the Parthenon in Greece, climbing the steps of the historic temple of Borobudur in Java, Indonesia, and gazing up at Diamond Head in Hawaii. He enjoyed driving across Canada with the family after we had been in Montreal for four days at EXPO '67.

Kathleen remarked that what she treasured was her childhood in the jungles of West Borneo, seeing the flora and fauna and the interaction of nature. She valued the ingenuity of her parents in managing a livelihood in an Asian setting, by adapting to local ways as much as it would prove safe and practical for the family. She has always appreciated strong ties with her siblings. She was very impressed with the cultural diversities of life in many parts of Indonesia. Because of her various experiences, she has a tender heart of compassion for the poor. She said that gaining independence and competence in her international travels and in her interaction with a variety of people was a priceless heritage.

She expressed herself so well in a recent email—taking highlights from Isaiah 55:1-4 and Isaiah 9:2 as follows:

I want something more. I am thirsty.
I want more of the sense of the presence of the Lord.

Come, all you who are thirsty, come to the waters;
come buy and eat without money and without cost,
your soul will delight in the richest of fare.
I will make an everlasting covenant with you,
My faithful love promised to David.

The people walking in darkness have seen a great light;
on those living in the shadow of death a light has dawned.
I know that faith comes by hearing the Word.
It is time for abundant sowing. I am hungry for that.
See I have made them a witness to the peoples.

Instead of possible trouble I see the gracious hand of God. I
came into this neighborhood longing for courage and love to
become a part of them. That it happened was no small thing.
There were many obstacles. But here, among a people who are
supposed to hate my kind of person, I stand as one of them.
And I feel the urgency of wanting them to be one of us.

Again! O God, do it again!
A cry, a longing,
A groan for them, for us.
Again! Do it again!

Each of our children had a spiritual new-birth experience in
their early years. At four years of age, Sylvia sat on my lap in an
Indonesian service and began to cry. I took her to a small room to
find out why. Amazingly, at that early age she felt bad because of
her sin. I prayed with her, and she found peace with God. After
that, praying with her for special needs was common. Tim had his
turning point with the Lord at spiritual-emphasis meetings in high
school, where his peers and teachers prayed with him.

During one of the children's Christmas vacations in Borneo, I
read parts of the life-story of Joseph every night. One evening
Richard was deeply touched. He empathized with the boy Joseph
who was rejected by his brothers and sold to Egyptian traders. We
talked about it and as we prayed together he found peace in his
own heart and mind. Kathleen committed her life to God at an
Indonesian youth camp, while her Dad was teaching on Dr.
Jaffray's sacrificial life.

On one return trip to Canada, we visited a large church in London, England, where we enjoyed a wonderful service. Sitting beside his Dad, Ken began to cry. Gordon took him to a quiet place to pray with him. At the end of the service Ken told the pastor that he'd received Jesus into his heart. He was just six years old. The above spiritual encounters were a good start for each of our children.

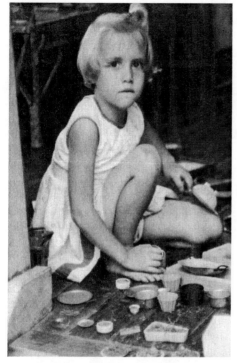

Sylvia, playing in Kelansam

Because each of our children is unique, their responses to life-experiences have been different. Ken became a very independent adventurer. Richard, the reader, having a private personality, often sought solitude. Kathleen, the pensive one, in her teens was touched by God to follow in her parents' footsteps. Tim preferred reading and computer skills to the social scene. Sylvia, our "little caboose", the compassionate one, found special solace in writing poetry and consoling lonely friends. In a book to my children I expressed myself in "reflections and appreciation" for each one, cherishing who they are and what they have become.

The above only partially describes our children's true identities, the purpose God had in mind when He created them. In their adult lives each one has found a special place of fulfillment in their careers, in their marriage relationships and in touching people for God.

In conclusion, how could missionary children glean the greatest advantage from experiences in a foreign country? How was their faith preserved? For us, as absentee parents, often the only recourse was prayer, much prayer and more prayer, crying to

God that the right people would be there for each one whenever they needed it. In the end, the vital constant was God's faithfulness as He walked with them, where we couldn't, through the difficult periods of their lives.

In preparation for planting, a water buffalo plows flooded rice paddies in Tana Toraja

CHAPTER 10

DESIGNATED FOR VICTORY

To think of our enemies as our best friends is a contradiction. When Joseph's brothers sold him to the Egyptian merchants, everything he held dear was taken away from him. His brothers could never have done him so much good with their love and favour as they did for him with their hatred and malice. However, it would take years for Joseph to realize God's plan in it. Is there redemptive value in a devastating loss? There is—if we give it to God with a thankful heart. The key is found in Hebrews 13:15a, "Through Jesus, therefore, let us offer to God a sacrifice of praise". A sacrifice is giving up something that is dearly held.

An old maxim states, "What you grasp you lose; what you give to God you gain." King Solomon confirmed this paradox in Proverbs 11:24a, "One man gives freely, yet gains even more." Jesus spoke in Matthew 10:39, "Whoever finds his life will lose it, and whoever loses his life for my sake will find it."

It is possible to be courageous and heroic in the face of disappointments. In fact, often our best learning experiences come not from successes, but from failure. Adversity introduces a man to himself. That is a scary thought, but we do grow stronger in adversity if God is in it. In our work, in whatever happened, we determined to obey our dear Lord. P.P. Bliss wrote:

Hold the fort for I am coming, Jesus signals still;
Wave the answer back to heaven, by Thy grace we will.

When Christ called His disciples there was no coercion. Jesus simply gave His simple summons, "Follow Me." When the Holy Spirit drew them face to face with the eternal God and His purpose, it became a clarion call they could not resist. Paul describes its long-term effect in Romans 8:35, 37, "Who shall separate us from the love of Christ? Shall trouble or hardship or persecution … or danger or sword? … No, in all these things we are more than conquerors through him who loved us."

In mid-1968 the next stage in our missionary journey was an assignment to East Indonesia. We were in Sumba for nine months, replacing a missionary couple who were on home leave. We learned the lifestyles and cultures of very a different people group compared to those of the Dyaks whom we had learned to love in West Borneo. It was an important transition. God wanted us to gain an understanding of the multicultural milieu of the Indonesian people we would be serving in the future years of our missionary work.

We discovered dear Christians in Sumba and Timor. God's working was evident in their lives. Churches were being planted. The believers considered their many church functions and cottage meetings very important, which created a cohesive social community. However, they lacked spiritual maturity.

Some of the churches had been revived by the miraculous ministries of Indonesian Christians that began in Soe, on the island of Timor. Though many nominal Christians had come to genuine faith in Christ, even destroying their fetishes and charms, some basic superstitions were still being carried over into everyday living. Sometimes they seemed more fascinated with what appeared to be miraculous manifestations and dreams than they were with scriptural truth. They needed consistent and balanced Bible teaching.

Our assignment was in district ministries. The mother church in Kambaniru and churches at Panda, Minggit Timbi and Mau Mau were in great need of spiritual guidance. Since they had no ordained minister on the island, Gordon served communion, baptized new believers and gave general direction to their church leaders.

Gordon attempted to visit the Waidjelu church 120 km away. On that trip they had to ford several rivers. He and his group never did get there. As he wrote in his conference report, "I never sank a boat in Kalimantan, but I sank a car in Sumba." When the back end of the car was dangerously submerged, water seeped into the gas tank. Once the car was back on land, Gordon found it very difficult to remove the water from the gas tank.

We were also involved in a lay training institute with a few young men from the islands of Alor, Timor, Sumba and Sumbawa. They learned the rudiments of the Christian faith. With that basic training they would be assigned to work in their district churches. Because one of the students had been trained to make bricks, his peers had the advantage of learning the trade from him after their morning classes.

During a trip to Waidjelu, Gordon Chapman recruits locals
to help him ford a river

The islands of Sumba, Timor, Alor and Flores just north of Australia, are volcanic. It wasn't uncommon to feel light tremors several times a month. Hills of limestone rock were visible evidence of eruptions in ages past. We lived on the island's dry, eastern side where it rained only about three months out of the whole year.

Hundreds of corn cobs complete with their husks, strung up in a continuous line on coconut trees were a conspicuous indication of their food storage. Layers of the rings of corn cobs surrounded the tree's trunk right to the top. As corn was needed, 20 cobs would be taken down. Its kernels had to be crushed in a mortar and pestle before it was ready for cooking. Corn and another kind of softer grain that didn't need to be crushed were their staple foods. Some tropical fruits and vegetables were also available. Coconuts were plenteous. Some of our produce came from the western part of the island where there was more rainfall and more vegetation.

Sap from the first stages of the fruit of the nipa palm tree, collected in the early morning, created a mildly sweet and deliciously nutritious drink. If it was boiled down at that stage, it became a tasty brown sugar candy. But that sap began its

121

fermentation process as soon as it was collected, eventually becoming palm wine. It was not uncommon to see men walking the streets at midday rather inebriated because they had been drinking nipa palm wine with added ingredients to make it even more intoxicating.

Every day men walked the streets selling palm wine in bamboo containers about four feet long and four and a half inches in diameter. It was commonly used in their feasts, though not everyone drank it. They revelled in the fact that, although they were poor, they could still celebrate every possible occasion with feasts.

The terrain in eastern Sumba was covered most of the year with dry grass, which was food for the cattle and horses. Wells were crucial for survival. As a result, Catholic leaders tended to give windmills (for pumping well water) to farmers if they signed up as followers of Catholicism. Viewing the prairie lands, the windmills presented a strong symbol of identity. Although windmills were not used in the city, wells were also a part of every dwelling place in the city. Besides its value for household use, well water provided an indispensable means for watering the homeowners' small gardens in the dry season.

Riding horseback was a common mode of transportation throughout the island. And annual horseback races were part of the island's entertainment. Horses were visible in every part of their local art and culture.

In our time at Jaffray Theological College one outstanding student from Sumba was Robert Mangi. After he graduated he returned to his people to become an esteemed regional director, strengthening the churches in this district, which included Sumba, Flores, Timor and Alor Islands. In time, a theological training school located in Kupang, Timor, the district's capital, had a significant influence in deepening the spirituality of believers. In Alor, training laymen for Christian work had been initiated soon after World War II. After we started teaching at Jaffray College, in Makassar, Gordon was invited to return to their district to teach the leaders more advanced biblical principles.

* * * * * * *

In mid-1969, we planned a special brief vacation with our children on the resort island of Bali. It was an added blessing to stay with colleagues, Ken and Carolyn Van Kurin. Gordon also helped Ken in the critical stages of the construction of the Denpasar Church.

During this time Bali was hosting the East Indonesia National Church Conference. With Gordon being so near and available, they asked him to provide daily devotional messages. Then, the conference committee decided to send a request to the Indonesian Alliance Missionary Conference in Bandung, requesting that they appoint us to teach at the Jaffray Theological College (STTJ) for the coming year. The Mission acceded to that request. Although we accepted the assignment with trepidation, eventually the challenge of teaching there proved to be an enjoyable experience.

Gordon Chapman handing out assignments to students
at Jaffray Theological College

However, since our household things and study materials were still stored in West Borneo near Sintang, we first had to take a quick trip to pick them up. That journey included our initial MAF plane flight from Pontianak to Sintang in 1969. From our lofty vantage point, during that one-hour flight, we recognized many familiar places and thanked God for allowing us to get an aerial view of our 15 years of service there.

We briefly renewed warm fellowship with some of our dear friends and colleagues. Earlier we had received a letter that was dated May 1968, in which the West Borneo District Conference had voted unanimously for us to return to serve them. They expressed sincere regrets because we were leaving their province.

To compensate for the loss, they invited us back for renewed fellowship times in the early 1980s to minister at a district youth camp. At that time some of our alumni came long distances to see us again. And in 1988 the Immanuel Bible School, where we had served for 12 years, invited Gordon to speak at their graduation and other related meetings. Keeping in touch with their growing work is a blessing to this day.

Upon arrival in Makassar in August 1969, we started teaching at STTJ, the college founded before the Second World War by Dr. Robert Jaffray. We were warmly welcomed by missionary colleagues, Maurice and Vi Bliss, and by the national Jaffray Theological College staff. In part we would be filling the gap left by Walter and Viola Post who had been moved to Bandung, Java.

Two years earlier, rioters in the city of Makassar had attacked and damaged 25 churches and two theological schools. At that time, all of the Jaffray Theological College records from 1930 to 1967 had been destroyed. Many instructional materials were also lost. Our lesson materials from Borneo had not yet arrived. We had to quickly find replacement lessons. This encouraged us to begin producing permanent teaching materials.

Gordon and I enjoyed teaching. Students called Gordon's teaching style creative, thought-provoking and scholarly. He presented truths with authority, integrity and sincerity, interspersing his teaching with humour to help them remember valuable lessons. Several of his students loved the freedom he gave them to question what he taught, which was a new experience for them—foreign to the Indonesian culture. Gordon wanted them to develop their own convictions about doctrinal truth and faith. That interaction benefited other classmates who did not have the courage to ask.

Gordon acquired his knowledge from a lifetime love of reading quality books. His prime interest was theology, but he also read fiction. General knowledge and new scientific findings always stimulated his thinking.

I loved to teach by drawing out students' reactions to scriptural truth. On one occasion, when presenting the teachings of Christ, I sensed that the students were intensely moved by the lesson. I stopped lecturing to give them time to seek God for their own personal needs. In their prayers it was obvious that they were making vital commitments for their future.

Soon after our arrival, we received requests for ministries beyond Jaffray College. The dean of the Foreign Languages

Academy, a school connected with The Paulus Christian University, asked me to teach conversational English and wanted Gordon to teach their religion classes. Previously, Walter Post had taught them. Since there were no restrictions in content, he could use Bible truth freely. This was a delightful challenge for him as students from different religious backgrounds faithfully attended classes throughout the school year. One of Gordon's students was a teacher from a nearby island who was a member of the majority religion. He was an attentive, thoughtful man who invited us to his home because he appreciated our friendship. One day he came to our house asking me for a Bible, assuring me that he was merely interested in reading it.

Adina Chapman teaching conversational English
to the professional community in Makassar

Gordon was also assigned to be the Academy's Chaplain, which meant he was to speak to the whole student body about once a month in a worship service. On one occasion, he referred to the topic of love in his message. Immediately a tittering arose. He sensed the vibes and had a great opportunity to explain the difference between sacrificial love in marriage, as ordained by God, and free sex, a self-serving act they understood completely.

Subsequently, Gordon was asked to speak at a Chinese youth camp where he was assigned a series of messages on Christian courtship and youth issues. Later he was asked to speak in a Makassar city church on Christian courtship and promiscuous relationships which often ended in abortion. A large part of his message was the Biblical view of abortion. When he later addressed these issues in a Jaffray College chapel message, his presentation shocked the student body and precipitated one-on-one discussions.

The dean of the foreign languages department of the main university in the city invited Gordon and me and Maurice Bliss to teach in their English upgrading classes. This opportunity gave us the added benefit of being involved with Makassar's professional people. Our students were doctors, professors, teachers and top military personnel. When Jaffray College investigated the possibility of becoming registered with the government, this opportunity provided a strategic contact. It was one of the participants in those classes who helped make that registration possible.

In the ESL classes, I taught English conversation and Gordon taught grammatical structure on a higher level. Once, in one of the classes, the students discussed the meaning of "clothes closet". Why would a closet have clothes? The only closet they knew was a WC—a water closet. It created a hilarious moment. In another class, as they were discussing eating in restaurants, Gordon asked them if they ever took their wives out to eat. They were amazed, for although they would take a female co-worker, they never took their wives.

In my classes I had opportunity to distribute *Decision* magazines and similar materials for extra reading. The Billy Graham Evangelistic Association sent me various past-issue Christian reading materials to give away. After reading a *Decision* magazine, one of my class members decided to order this periodical for all the pastors of a synod in his church organization. At that time we were also free to have lively debates concerning social and Christian ethical issues.

Another extra ministry in which Gordon and Maurice Bliss shared preaching responsibilities was a weekly English worship service. These meetings reached professional people who had an interest in upgrading their English language skills. Sixteen years earlier, while we were in language study in 1953, we had had a vital part in Lawrence Kamasi's life when he attended these services.

As a university graduate, Lawrence had been offered a government scholarship to study in the U.S.—a privilege many college graduates coveted. But when Lawrence heard John

Kleinpeter speak in revival meetings in the mother church in Makassar, he was deeply convicted of his sinful state before a holy God and he accepted Christ as his Saviour. At the same time, the Lord called him to serve Him for the rest of his life. For Lawrence, it was a very hard decision. His father was devastated with his plans, saying he wouldn't give his son any money if he gave up his U.S. scholarship. But the call of God was so strong on his life that he could do nothing other than obey his Master. At that time, because he requested counselling, we played a vital role in helping him make his decision.

The Indonesian C&MA missionaries then arranged a scholarship for Lawrence to study at Ebenezer Bible College in Zamboanga City, Philippines. He was also quite involved in preparing Indonesian Christian radio programs at the FEBC station in Manila. When he came back to Indonesia, he became teacher and Director of the Jaffray Theological College. His students highly respected him for his engaging teaching style. Later he received a Mission scholarship to take his doctoral studies at Fuller Theological Seminary in Pasadena, California. On returning to Makassar he continued his responsibilities at the Jaffray College and was also elected to be the first president of the C&MA's national organization, GKII.

We benefited so much from our friendship with Rev. Kamasi, for he understood us well. Unfortunately, when his older children were only in their teens he succumbed to cancer. Though he was taken early in life, he left behind an abiding legacy for all who knew him.

We were also greatly blessed when Rev. Chavan from our India National Alliance Church came to hold special meetings at Jaffray College. His ministry blessed Christians in some of our city churches as well as in other provinces in Indonesia.

Another guest speaker was Rev. Paul Bartel, former Alliance missionary to China and Hong Kong. In 1971, this pioneer missionary's messages and life example gave our Jaffray College students a new view of a Christian's commitment to service. Though he was retired, Paul visited Chinese churches in several Far East countries one more time. In Makassar his messages blessed a large Chinese church fellowship that had been a part of The Chinese Foreign Missionary Union, Dr. Jaffray's organization of Chinese pastors, who came to work with their people in Indonesia. As a guest in our home, Rev. Bartel's visit brought back a flood of memories of his parent's visit on our Saskatchewan farm during my childhood.

* * * * * * *

Frequently we were involved in youth ministries. In 1970, during the long school vacation, Vi Bliss, the director for youth ministries at the first GKII national church in Makassar, asked Gordon to give the devotional messages at a youth camp she had organized. Vi also asked me to teach a class every day.

In addition to my teaching responsibilities at Jaffray College, I provided devotional messages at Christian Women's Fellowship meetings throughout the year and special messages for their Christmas and Easter rallies. Our slide presentations at Christmas and Easter Sunday school rallies brought many new children to their Sunday schools.

After the Blisses left for furlough, the youth work in the GKII first church in Makassar was assigned to me. I prepared and directed a Christmas drama, with Anne Moore assisting in the music. It ended with all the actors kneeling at the foot of a large cross on the platform in a symbolic presentation of their surrender to Christ. This truth, that Jesus came to earth as an infant to ultimately die for the salvation of mankind, was a focus that had not been mentioned in a Christmas drama to this audience before.

Gordon was also asked to provide devotional messages at a May 1971 Chinese youth camp, with topics especially related to current moral youth issues. In a letter of thanks on behalf of the organizing committee, Evangelist Lucia Tjoa reported: "We witnessed how the Holy Spirit worked in the hearts of our young people. They have determined to live for Christ. Of the 75 participants, 17 young people surrendered their lives to service for God. Our young people were deeply blessed by your teaching from God's Word."

Gordon wrote, "I have never seen Christmas celebrated as much as in Makassar. I fear that with so much celebration the heart and true meaning of Christmas escapes many people." In every church the women's fellowship, the youth group and the Sunday school each had their own celebration. It was always difficult to fulfill all the calls for ministry. Requests came from the churches where Alliance workers had been known for many years, as well as from offices and business connections who wanted to celebrate Christmas with their staff and their friends. As a result, we observed a more complete view of the influence of Christianity in Makassar and in the province.

* * * * * * *

At Jaffray College we needed spiritual renewal. Too many problems surfaced day after day. In his 1971 conference report, referring to difficulties which the national church experienced within the general population, the Mission chairman spoke of the "Makassar upheaval in 1967". He mentioned that although "the problems had not evaporated, they no longer dominated the national church scene." Although they didn't dominate the scene in our time, issues in the neighbourhood still simmered and flared up from time to time. Sometimes stones were hurled at our campus buildings causing considerable agitation. There were times when students had to be on guard all night because of disturbances in the area surrounding our campus.

However, immediate internal issues were even more explosive in the 1970/71 school year. Gordon had been asked to be the student advisor for the Teachers' Committee. One day he was challenged with a student rebellion. A scathing letter had been written and signed by some of the students in which they rejected a certain teacher. Gordon dealt with them firmly saying that some things they had written were not Christ-like. They softened their injurious remarks before presenting the letter in a staff meeting.

Gordon was asked to follow up on the complaints and to investigate the roots of the dispute. To determine their personal feelings in the matter, he talked to the students involved individually. Without their being previously informed of his intent, he simply called them out of class one-by-one for these discussions. This process generated good results.

Students who had participated in making written allegations against the teacher then volunteered to call a reconciliation meeting, asking the two missionary couples on staff to be present as witnesses. When the teacher who had been accused arrived, he went to the podium and accepted the students' individual apologies. After that, one by one the students followed their confessions with passionate prayers for God's intervention in their future. This was a miraculous preparation for their Christian service for the coming days. It had been their decision. It was their victory. Thirty years later we heard from them by email, describing their various leadership assignments.

Dr. Jacob Tomatala and his wife now live in Jakarta. Dr. Tomatala was chosen to be the Director of the Jaffray College's extension in the capital city of Jakarta. Later, he brought that school under independent administration, naming it the Jaffray Institute of Philosophy, Theology and Leadership Jakarta. The Institute provides undergraduate, graduate and postgraduate studies. Dr. Tomatala has written ten books related to his work. His wife, Magdalena, has also authored a book.

In a May 1998 Asia-Pacific Alliance Conference in Taipei, Dr. Tomatala was deeply moved for his country-men. In a small group, Rev. Jim Kendall, Director of the Alliance Mission in Jakarta, joined Dr. Tomatala as he prayed a passionate prayer, confessing to God that, though he had hated people in his country for burning 24 churches in the past year—even burning one pastor alive, he realized that Jesus loved them enough to die for them. Though he had taught missions for years, he had never taught his students to love those people. He had a new understanding of Christ's fathomless love for all men.

At the July 2001 GKII National Assembly, the delegates elected Dr. Tomatala as President for the 2001 to 2003 period, and his wife, Magdalena, as National President of Alliance Women. They face many challenges in the new era. They know that they cannot manage those responsibilities without much prayer support as they address the political and economic uncertainties in their large, religiously diverse country.

When Magdalena came from Sumba for her first year of studies at Jaffray College, we received her like an adopted daughter. She became a wonderful mother and teacher. In August 2000, when the Indonesian Alliance Women celebrated their 13th anniversary, their conference banner read, "Prepare for a Great Harvest in the New Millennium". She challenged the women saying, "This is a time of great turmoil for the Indonesian nation. Probably things will be even more difficult in days to come. We must witness to others about our faith while we still have freedom to do so." Those were compelling words for the delegates of Alliance Women from the seven districts of the GKII national organization. They never imagined that just four months later, thousands of Christians in Indonesia would be traumatized.

Christmas Eve 2000 will long be remembered by Indonesian Christians as a day of destruction and death. At least 18 bombs were detonated near churches, seminaries or parsonages in Jakarta and in eight other cities throughout Indonesia. Hundreds were injured, and more than a hundred died. Christian leaders urged their members to forgive as Christ had taught them to forgive. Many people turned to God for stronger faith. It was reported that none of our GKII national churches were directly hit.

Another student dissenter, Rev. John Dana, became a teacher at Jaffray College after he graduated. Later he moved to Java to become director of another theological school majoring in church planting, which he eventually registered as The Good News Foundation. In his email to me he said:

> I claim you as my spiritual parents. I respected you for your deep sincerity in your teaching and in your lives. You helped me to be the servant God intended me to be. I am still using ideas in my renewal messages that you taught me.
>
> On November 15, 1978, together with my assistants, we organized The Christian Bible Church of Indonesia. We now have 200 evangelists that are diligently planting churches in 14 Indonesian provinces. We are praying that God will guide us in our target of planting 450 new churches in the 1994 to 2004 time period.

In April 2000 he reported that the Central Government party members of fundamental Muslim, Hindu and Buddhist persuasion demanded that strict religious laws be reinstated. Such laws would forbid followers of one religion to become followers of another religion. This edict would make the work of evangelists and pastors punishable by law in Indonesia, hindering them from reaching 80 percent of the country's population. When this ruling was established, Rev. Dana encouraged his workers to obey God rather than man and to be ready to face the consequences. Rev. Dana is a frequent speaker at church seminars and conferences.

Rev. Markus G. Tembang, the man who led the student protest in 1971, was not in the reconciliation meeting that followed. But in 1996 I received a brochure of the dedication of their newly completed Antioch Fellowship house of worship. When he completed his studies and was ready for Jaffray College's internship program, he was invited by the Jakarta national church to plant the Antioch Fellowship in a Jakarta suburb. In his brochure he inserted a letter to me saying that I would probably never believe that God could bless him.

He had been renewed and God had anointed him for ministry. When he graduated from Jaffray College his Jakarta synod assigned him as pastor of the Antioch Fellowship for several more years. Then for the next ten years he was called to pastor the First National Church in Jakarta. In his absence the Antioch Fellowship faced some rocky times, actually being without a pastor for a year. When he returned in 1987 God strengthened the fellowship again, and they were able to proceed with building a permanent worship centre, which they dedicated in 1996.

Rev. Yakob Ungking was one of the faithful interim leaders whom God blessed at the Antioch Fellowship. [He was not in the 1971 protest movement at Jaffray College.] He and his wife had come from the West Borneo national church fellowship. Rev. Ungking had his theological training in West Borneo and in Jaffray College, in Makassar. He served the Lord well until his sudden death in 1986.

Rev. Hendrik Jakob served as a faithful teacher and Director of the Walter Post Theological College, in Sentani, Irian Jaya (Papua New Guinea). For years he and his wife Kristine taught in this province so far away from their own people. Hendrik and Kristine were both present in the 1971 student rebellion and reconciliation meeting. Recently, together with a missionary couple, Hendrik has been teaching intensive upgrading discipleship and leadership training courses, targeting interior Papuan pastors for renewal ministries.

Dr. Gideon Tandirerung received a scholarship to study in Manila. He subsequently became a teacher at Jaffray College. Among other things, he later served as an evangelist. There were other students in that reconciliation meeting who are also faithfully serving the Lord. If all their stories were told it would surely affirm God's renewing power because of their obedience to Him. Together they are a part of the great army of Christian leaders who are *embracing the mountain* for Christ's Kingdom.

* * * * * * *

We received letters from both missionary and national church brethren regarding some challenges. Often at issue were the cultural differences. Westerners, though very sincere, seemed too forthright. On the other hand, as one dear Indonesian pastor explained the Indonesian approach, the more difficult the topic, the longer the preamble in addressing it. Our Indonesian brethren solved problems and made decisions on the basis of consensus. An Indonesian proverb says, "There is no ivory which is not cracked," meaning that no man is without faults. How people deal with inequities in interpersonal relationships in Christian ministry is a challenge in any country.

Confronted with so many new cultural learning experiences in Indonesia, Gordon and I were exhausted. Then a compassionate Indonesian brother encouraged us by saying, "As I see it you must not give up but you should return to serve us. If you do not return, the wrong attitudes of my Indonesian brothers will be considered right. No good can come of it. Just keep trusting God and return to serve us."

At this critical time Dr. Richard Harvey's ministry had a profound renewal influence on us and on our college. Remembering that event, Dr. Peter Anggu, Director of Jaffray College wrote:

> When Dr. Richard Harvey visited our college, Gordon was assigned to translate for him. It was a very unusual experience for me. I had never felt the Holy Spirit's presence in such a powerful way. It revived the atmosphere all over our campus." [Dr. Harvey had used illustrations from his book, *Seventy Years of Miracles*, to strengthen the teaching in his messages. –a.c.]
>
> For as long as I have been at Jaffray Theological College I have passionately longed for an awakening by the Holy Spirit like that among us. Why was it so urgent at that time? — because we needed Him so desperately. The power of God settled so many disturbing problems. After those God-encountering experiences I observed that students and teachers alike willingly showed an openness with one another until there were no more conflicting issues.
>
> When I have presented the need of a mighty Holy-Spirit awakening on our campus, it's that 1972 divine movement I remember. I long for a similar spiritual awakening to solve our many unmanageable difficulties.

After that event, Dr. Anggu would still have another 20 years of God-anointed leadership ministry at Jaffray Theological College.

In 1973, when we returned to Indonesia after our home service, one of the things we enjoyed was a special one-year assignment at our church's national publication office in Bandung,

Java. After that, we would be assigned to work alongside wonderful Christian leaders and their tribal people of mountainous Torajaland. With them we would experience precious fellowship for another 18 years. During most of our time in Torajaland, we also taught at Jaffray Theological College in Makassar. That was the victory awaiting us in our remaining years of service in Indonesia. Our Conqueror was in charge. The blessings of it are expressed in the chorus of the following song:

Victory ahead! Victory ahead!
Thro' the blood of Jesus, victory ahead;
Trusting in the Lord, I hear the Conqueror's tread,
By faith I see the victory ahead.

—Rev. William Grum

Craig & Bev Hendrikson, Adina Chapman and daughter, Kathleen
rest in the shade of a small Toraja house.
This size of building was often used to store rice.

CHAPTER 11

KIBAID PERSPECTIVES

KIBAID is an Indonesian acronym that means "Indonesian Gospel Fellowship" (IGF). The homeland of this fellowship is the province of Toraja in the highlands of South Sulawesi, Indonesia. Often excelling in their pursuits, the Torajanese became founders, builders and entrepreneurs. They set their sights on possibilities within the larger community rather than on problems.

In pursuing higher education, many of them became doctors, lawyers, professors, government workers, business administrators, policemen and military personnel. Along with starting churches in their home province of Toraja, their Christian leaders also developed strong fellowship groups in the city of Makassar. Their unique strengths were fittingly transferred into ministry for the Kingdom of God.

We were awed by the beauty of the pastoral scenes in the rugged highland province of Toraja. The air is often crisp and cool. Survival in that environment has developed a zealous, loving people. Learning to understand their cultural uniqueness was a very rewarding experience. Many of their believers became dedicated Christian workers.

In a typical Torajanese village the roofs of their houses are replicas of the structure of a boat, reflecting their peoples' possible origin. It is said that their ancestors arrived on boats. The main Torajanese house stands high on stilts with rather limited living space. Beside it stands a second house, similar in construction, which is used for their annual rice storage. Its lower level has an open platform used as a work place and a rest area where friends come to enjoy a visit. Though most people in the province now live in simple dwelling places, nobility often have the two artistically built Toraja house structures side by side, with a more modern home beside it.

Managing the transitions of life and death in Torajaland is fundamental to their culture. Understanding the exclusive features of how they treat their deceased loved ones is vital to getting acquainted with the Torajanese tribe. Tourists visit Toraja to witness the traditional celebration of the "Feast for the Dead". In October 1973 we had an opportunity to view these extravagant and complex rites. This event had specifically been planned to begin the deification of three noblemen. Sometimes bodies of deceased loved ones are preserved and kept for years, waiting for the occasion when important relatives can all be present for the ceremony.

It took months of hard work to prepare the site for this ceremony. Three sides of a large field were enclosed by U-shaped bamboo buildings consisting of 49 sections. The funeral pavilion where the deceased loved ones would be laid in state for the 3-day event was an elaborate Toraja house structure in the centre of the field. A reliable estimate, at that time, put the cost of its construction at around $50,000 Cdn.

The day before the ceremonies began, a festively decorated water buffalo passed by our house. As a gift, it honoured the three deceased noblemen and their families. (Symbolically, the buffalo is the mount for the dead. In the animistic belief of the Torajanese, the buffalo is also the guardian for the dead. They must honour their dead loved ones with all due respect to give them the right of passage to the next life, for they believe that the spirits of dead ancestors watch over the living to bless or to curse them.)

The following day a procession came by with coffins in Toraja-house biers. Between these biers was a sedan chair covered in black cloth, carrying the widows and sisters of the deceased men. The biers and the sedan chair balanced on long bamboo poles which about 30 men carried on their shoulders. Every 50 yards or so the carriers stopped, performed a dance and then continued the carrying process. An honour guard of four glassy-eyed dancers preceded the procession. They performed the Ma'rinding Dance—a war dance in which they flourished spears and shields—symbolic of war dances in past tribal warfare. Accompanying this distinguished ceremony, they transported the mourners the five kilometre distance to the festivity site. There they placed the coffins in the funeral pavilion in the centre of the U-shaped structure of bamboo buildings.

The Ma'rinding Dancers also preceded each entourage of extended family members or friends who came as guests to present their gifts of live pigs or water buffalo. Some women brought gifts of grain or eggs. The guests were paraded around the periphery of the field, ending at the funeral pavilion in the centre of the arena. Then they ascended the upper section where the noblemen were lying in state. The deceased men were Puang Mendedek Andi Lolo, Puang Lai' Kelua' and Puang So' Rerung. A banner above the house declared, "Pesanan Terachir: 'Pegang teguh Kesatuan Kita, Terlebih Dalam Keluarga.'" (translated, "A last message: 'Hold fast to our unity, especially within the family.'")

As guests were received, their gifts of live animals were carefully recorded. These offerings became a debt to the families of the deceased. They would have to repay in kind when the donors experienced a death in their families. This act created within the tribe the perpetual obligation that they called their "Unity in the Family".

After the guests had paid their respects they were ushered to one of the many sections in the two-level bamboo structures for accommodating visitors. The animals they brought were usually ceremonially killed and then cooked to feed the thousands of guests who attended. The carriers received special parts of the animals they had transported.

When the guests first arrived, long lines of young women dressed in black were always on hand to serve them snacks and drinks. Then the guests spent endless hours visiting friends and family and eating the special foods prepared for them. Food was served on banana leaves, and their "disposable cups" were sections of bamboo. In their animistic culture, the "Feast for the Dead" was the most important socializing time for the tribe.

Gordon, and a friend, photographed the festivities. As they left, an afternoon drizzle produced a beautiful rainbow. The symbolism of the rainbow in the sky was overshadowed by the animistic futility they had observed. The rainbow's meaning and message of God's preservation and redemption had escaped these people. They were too deeply involved in the vital ceremonies deifying the deceased noblemen.

The remains of the noblemen were then carried to a burial site, which rose high up in the sheer limestone cliffs. These cliffs, honeycombed with caves, were used as tombs. More recently, caves have been laboriously carved out of the limestone cliffs for the wealthy or aristocratic people. After the coffins were sealed they were hoisted up a bamboo ladder to their resting place high above ground. Clothed, hardwood effigies of the deceased loved ones were placed in a gallery near the cave. Annually these effigies would be given new clothes. The remains of poorer people were usually placed in caves at the base of the cliffs in family-type plots,—"So that they can enjoy each other in the afterlife".

Perched high on limestone cliffs, hard-wood effigies of the Torajanese dead stand guard over their gravesite

To respect this traditional cultural custom, an "Alternate Christian Feast" was prepared by Mr. Pasak and his wife. As a respected businessman and an elder of the mother church in the Toraja Indonesian Gospel Fellowship, Mr. Pasak had himself experienced a glorious release from the powers of darkness. The transformation of his life was most visible in his bright eyes and the glow on his face.

To witness the celebration of his father Ika's passage from spirit worship to Christianity, they invited extended family members and numerous guests, celebrating this Christian event. They sold eight live water buffalo and presented the proceeds to civil authorities in their city, as was the custom. The purpose of this feast was to absolve all who participated in the celebration of any future debts. Mr. Pasak and his Christian wife prepared this feast in lieu of the "Unity in the Family" ceremony.

Many nominal Christians have never dealt with this phase of their belief. Their foreign church leaders did not believe in spirit worship, so they didn't initiate a change in their cultural lifestyle. But the IGF leaders taught their believers about deliverance from fear and endless ritual sacrifices, which were designed to appease the spirits. They believed that Jesus saved people from sin, that He sanctified them to be liberated from the bondage of all fear in spirit-worship, that He could heal believers and that He would come again to take us to heaven. Jesus was our Saviour, Sanctifier, Healer and Coming King—the message of the C&MA logo.

Having experienced their former celebrations of the "Feast for the Dead", it was actually an easy transition for the Torajanese Christians of the Indonesian Gospel Fellowship to organize 3-day annual Christmas youth rallies. In December 1973 they invited unbelievers from neighbouring villages to one day of their 3-day celebration. Their main purpose was to introduce them to the wonderful salvation in Jesus Christ. On that day they provided a feast for 3,000 people. Though Christians spent all morning preparing the food, amazingly, in just over one hour all 3,000 people were fed by using banana-leaf plates and bamboo-section cups.

Wrapped in sarongs to ward off the mountain chill, Torajanese tribes people arrive from miles around to take part in the annual Christmas Youth Festival

Choral groups from many IGF churches sang Christian songs. With bamboo instruments, different groups played their typical tribal Christian music. And many IGF leaders provided special messages. It was a privilege for us and the Craig Hendrickson family to be invited to share in this great celebration.

* * * * * * *

141

In their 1986 fiftieth anniversary celebration, the Indonesian Gospel Fellowship commemorated their victories over the challenges of forming their organization. They had to contend with opposition in the earlier days of their evangelistic outreach. Fundamentally, they emphasized that the first step in a Christian's life was to repent of one's sins and to receive Christ as Saviour.

The founders of the IGF, Rev. J. La'lang in Makassar city, and Rev. B. Bokko upcountry in Torajaland, were graduates of Dr. Jaffray's School of Theology in the early 1930s. It was Rev. Pouw Peng Hong (P.H. Pouw), Dr. Jaffray's colleague, who suggested that they use the name Indonesian Gospel Fellowship for their organization. This designated their understanding of the Great Commission mandate, which was to reach out to neighbouring tribes as well as to their own Torajanese people.

Fortunately, in their internship years, the founders of the IGF had experienced evangelistic outreach to the people in Sarawak (Malaysian Borneo) and in East Borneo, Sumatra and Java in Indonesia. In 1940 Rev. Bokko was assigned to accompany an Alliance missionary to work in Papua New Guinea. But because World War II had come to their country, the trip had to be cancelled. Rev. Bokko recognized the cancellation as God's plan so that he could return to evangelize his people in Toraja.

While farming in his home village of Burake he began to share the Good News with family and friends. He also did some evangelizing in nearby villages whose people were members of the Indonesian branch of the Dutch Reformed Church. December 1947 was a significant time when Rev. Bokko's Burake Fellowship began an intense evangelistic outreach to their extended family members and friends. Though pastors of the Dutch Reformed Church begged him to return to their group, he declined, saying that God wanted to establish the IGF in Burake.

The local Netherlands Indies Civil Administration opposed Rev. Bokko's purposes, causing much disturbance among the people of his congregation. However, with persistent prayer and one-on-one witnessing, the IGF continued to grow. Later, together with a colleague from Toraja, Rev. Bokko presented his case to the Department of Justice in Makassar. Their observation was that Rev. Bokko's fellowship was an indigenous, progressive and peaceful group. Permission was granted to pursue their goals.

As the IGF reached out to the south, north, east and west in Torajaland, they compared their growth with the events recorded in the book of Acts. As a result, in 1950, Rev. Bokko felt the urgency to start a Bible school upcountry in Makale to prepare pastors and evangelists for the IGF. Rev. P.G.T. Sallipadang, who was one of the first graduates of that Bible school, later became the second president of IGF.

Another major conflict arose when Kahar Muzakkar, leader of the Darul Islamic Movement, had the goal of enforcing syariah law in Toraja, making it a strict Muslim state. During that time the church suffered severe persecution, often forcing fellowship groups into hiding. Rev. Bokko visited them faithfully, and their work grew immensely.

The IGF also suffered much during the Japanese occupation during World War II, especially in Makassar. Eventually Rev. Bokko together with Rev. J. La'lang, President of the IGF from its inception, made a formal request to The East Indonesia Department of Justice to have their organization legally registered. On November 11, 1949 that permit was granted. Rev. La'lang's venerable leadership, which began in 1936, ended when he died in 1972.

Though the IGF had some setbacks, their progress was remarkable. They reached out to various tribes in their province of Toraja, to areas of Central Sulawesi, to Sabah in Malaysia, to Indonesian East Borneo, to the Maluku islands, to several cities in Java, and eventually to the cities of Jayapura and Merauke in Papua New Guinea. Often, as their lay people were transferred to job assignments in these various places, they used it as a bridge to begin church fellowships.

Through it all, the IGF considered themselves a sister organization of the GKII. Many IGF leaders are graduates of Jaffray College in Makassar. Several of the Torajanese students who graduated became teachers at Jaffray College. In fact, Dr. Peter Anggu, long-time President of Jaffray College, was a faithful Torajanese colleague of ours.

It is impossible to express how much Gordon and I cherished our fellowship in the gospel with numerous leaders of the IGF. Through the years, many of them were our colleagues and many of their people were our students. Rev. Titus Sampe was one of our students, who became their President in 1996. He had been a recipient of the Gordon Chapman Memorial Scholarship. At their momentous "Millennium 2000 Celebration" in Makassar, his challenging message to the assembly was "Launch out into the Deep", an encouragement to his people to accept the critical possibilities of the new millennium. It was reminiscent of Dr. A. B. Simpson's inspiring song, the second verse of which reads:

But many, alas! only stand on the shore,
And gaze on the ocean so wide;
They never have ventured its depths to explore
Or to launch on the fathomless tide.

Chorus:
Launch out into the deep and let the shoreline go,
Launch out, launch out in the ocean divine,
Out where the full tides flow.

Rev. Sampe added:

The era of our last four years has been very difficult. In the recent past our nation has suffered greatly because of economic, political and religious crises. It has caused unprecedented turbulence... A lot of things are trying to destroy the unity of our nation. ... In view of these issues, our future will demand much sacrifice. ... The potentials of the IGF's future will depend on how we face our difficulties by uniting our people in common goals. ... What will we establish as our responsibility for the 2000 to 2004 period to help the people we will reach through the members of the IGF?

As we face opportunities to express our faith, we must willingly serve our Lord in the love of Christ. We need to enhance our work programs in worship, in evangelism, in teaching, in administration, in partnerships with other evangelical organizations, in programs for our retirees, in managing our finances and in developing a constitution for our organization. These manifold advances can only be achieved with seminars and teaching ministries for all of our personnel in the IGF programs.

Jesus' charge to Peter in Luke 5:4b, 6a is for us. "Launch out into the deep and let down your nets for a draught ... when they had this done, they enclosed a great multitude of fishes" (KJV) In this new era let us launch out into new fields like Nabire in Papua, in Bali, and in Yogyakarta and Surabaya in Java. But none of this will happen unless we have well-qualified servants to do it. We must all do our part as we launch out into the deep for Jesus Christ. Then God's blessings will surely follow.

Ordained pastors of the IGF, many of them our alumni and later our colleagues in ministry, are key leaders today. Serving together with us daily for long periods were Dr. Peter Anggu, Rev. P.G.T. Sallipadang, Dr. Sadrak Kurang, Rev. B.R.S. Tinggi and Rev. P.S. Mangi. Miss Ludia Sumule Tinggi was a dear sister in the Lord whom I trained in library science skills. If all the stories of the IGF workers were told, it would certainly prove that they are a strategic part of a divinely appointed army who are standing hand in hand to *embrace the mountain* for God's Kingdom in Indonesia.

Rev. Zakaria Gojang compiled a very informative, KIBAID media information magazine for their July 2000 Millennium Celebration. He called it *The Supreme Mission of the Indonesian Gospel Fellowship*. More than a magazine, it was a vital history of the IGF's work. For me, it was a great encouragement to read. We also received a shorter 12-page brochure prepared for the IGF's Fiftieth Anniversary, which reported their courageous beginnings.

God had prepared us for our closer association with the Torajanese people. Beginning in mid-1973 we were assigned to teach in their Makale Theological School. There we also assisted in a variety of district ministries. Gordon participated in their Palopo regional Executive Committee meetings, where they especially asked him for consultation on pastoral transfers. I was asked to be the main speaker at their district-wide ladies' retreat.

Previously, in February 1973, while in Canada, God prepared my own heart for better days ahead in a spiritual renewal experience. As Oswald Chambers said in his *My Utmost for His Highest* devotional, "God will see that you have any number of opportunities to prove to yourself the marvels of His grace. ... You will never cease to be the most amazed person on earth at what God has done for you on the inside." In the months that followed that promise became very true for me in how I weathered the transition at that time and how I dealt with numerous health problems.

For all of November and part of December I suffered extensive asthma problems. In January a potential heart problem surfaced. A local doctor suggested I go to Makassar for more detailed care. I was hospitalized there for three weeks. During my recovery Gordon was able to assist Anne Moore in the production of several audio cassettes of Bible choruses she composed called *Koor-koor Alkitabiah*, for which she trained choral groups to sing.

After I was discharged from the hospital, Gordon returned to Makale, while I remained in Makassar under doctor's observation. During my convalescence I had amazing opportunities to counsel people one-on-one. They came to me where I was resting, sitting in Vonnie Morscheck's cool screened-in veranda. It was an encouraging ministry in my recovery time. In May I was able to join Gordon in Makale again.

The most significant event in our work with the dear IGF brethren upcountry came in 1974 when the board of the Makale Bible School asked Gordon to assist them in their land purchase. Plans continued to be blocked until late November when the committee located an ideal piece of property across the street from the First IGF Church in that city. Since the owner needed instant cash, it was being sold for a very favourable price.

Finances for the land purchase were limited. A down payment of $1,207 Cdn was needed by the first of December. The total indebtedness would be an added amount of 22 water buffalo—the local equivalent of gold as a medium of exchange. We loaned them $500 for the down payment. Their total debt was actually $2,360 Cdn. Some mission funds were donated. Six months later they repaid the $500 they had borrowed from us. The dedication of that new property was a great celebration time. Later, when an extra plot of land bordering their property became available they purchased it also.

By 1975 the IGF had built temporary buildings on their land. Classrooms, a dormitory, kitchen and dining room buildings were constructed of bamboo and thatch. They laid 300 metres of bamboo pipe to carry spring water down from the mountain, and erected the frame for a teacher's residence. It was a simple beginning.

After that, because of the death of an ordained pastor and the loss of a second pastor in Toraja, the church leaders decided to send some of their experienced pastors to Jaffray College in Makassar for upgrading courses for a year. The IGF Executive Committee added special subjects to prepare them for their ordination. Meanwhile senior students from the Makale Bible School were taken out of class to fill the pastoral vacancies.

Gordon carried a heavy workload of teaching assignments in the Makale Bible School. He taught 13 class hours a week. Two of his courses had no lesson material, so he started translating from his own library, beginning with books on the Pauline Epistles.

Mr. Biring, a Torajanese high school teacher in Makassar, willingly shared his excellent editing skills.

One day while I was walking to school on the narrow, slippery ridge between rice paddies, I took one wrong step and fell into the flooded paddy. My lesson book was badly soaked. I got up and brushed off some of the mud. I was in no state to stand in front of a class to teach, but the female students kindly came to my aid and provided me with a dry sarong.

Our house in Makale (centre), nestled in a peaceful mountainous landscape, over-looking a carpet of rice paddies

I also prepared devotional materials for the Makale youth group and for their ladies' fellowship meetings. For the next ladies' retreat I began preparing simple lessons on Ephesians, which they also used in their monthly newsletter. Rev. Mangi, who coordinated the Bible School's Christian service program, had students out every weekend preaching and teaching Sunday school. With colourful Bible story pictures from outdated Christian calendars, I prepared flash cards for Sunday school teachers and for evangelistic outreach ministries. I also provided a handbook to help pastors' wives in their responsibilities.

In one noteworthy ministry, the Makale Bible School provided dependable workers for the GKII church-plant program on Java Island. From its inception several evangelists have served in Java faithfully.

During that time I was afflicted with several illnesses. One fever incapacitated me. It was not a simple malarial fever. It could have been hepatitis. When improvement didn't come with local medical help, Gordon took me to Makassar. Dick and Barbara Smith graciously provided housing for more than three weeks while we were there. Gordon used that time to continue his translations. When we returned to Makale, Gordon resumed teaching while I convalesced until June 1974.

Because I didn't recover sufficiently, we left earlier than planned for our field conference in Java so that I could get medical help in Bandung. At our conference, providentially, Gordon was assigned to a fulfilling year-long ministry as liaison for the national church's Word of Life Publishing House. Because I had to have gallbladder surgery shortly after the conference and since the surgeon ordered a year's rest for me, it was an added blessing for us to be in the cool mountain climate of Bandung.

The surgeon had been most alarmed at my badly damaged liver. He said it was all grey and white. And because his surgery was poorly performed, I suffered abdominal pains for four years. During that time I still carried on my ministry as I was able. Finally in 1979, in Penang, Malaysia, an American doctor at the Seventh-day Adventist Hospital made extensive adhesion repairs. Thankfully, the surgery, plus guided therapy, got me back on my feet.

Back to 1976—as we were preparing for home service, the Makale Bible School Director urged us to come back on staff again when we returned. We deeply appreciated the acceptance and love of the IGF Christian community in Toraja and were especially blessed to be able to teach in their Bible school. When it was apparent that for health reasons I would not be able to live upcountry, Rev. Sallipadang, president of the IGF, said that if we couldn't return to Makale they had other work they wanted us to do. In God's time we enjoyed many more years of ministry with them in their Makassar churches, while simultaneously teaching at Jaffray Theological College.

* * * * * * *

Although we returned to teach at Jaffray College, our connections with the brethren in Makale did not end. When the Toraja IGF pastors invited Mr. Wiwcharuck for a strategic five-day seminar, Gordon had the privilege of accompanying him as translator. Mr. Wiwcharuck, of the United States Military, had developed excellent materials in leadership management. After he retired, he adapted these materials for seminars on Christian leadership. The Torajanese pastors desired leadership training. A total of 227 workers, church elders and students enjoyed Mr. Wiwcharuk's lectures. Reflecting on their mutual benefits, both the participants and Mr. Wiwcharuck referred to that time as the largest, most engaging training session ever.

In November of that year Mr. Mangi, Director of the Makale Bible School, once again invited Gordon to minister at a five-day retreat for all of the upcountry pastors and evangelists. Evening services were open to the Christian community in the city. The following week Gordon fulfilled a long-standing promise to the school by installing 50 metres of metal pipe, replacing the temporary bamboo conduits the school had been using to bring spring water down from the mountains nearby.

On December 27, Gordon was the special speaker at Makale Bible School's graduation, followed by the commissioning service of all the students and most of the teachers of the Bible school. They would be going out on evangelistic trips throughout their church region for 10 to 14 days. Several days later Gordon was the main speaker at a church dedication service.

Every year in late December, the IGF hosted the annual 3-day Christmas Youth Festival. Gordon spoke at several of these rallies. He enjoyed speaking to young people. They were always challenged by his timely messages. Young people from all of the IGF's upcountry churches, as well as those from Makassar and other south Sulawesi cities made every effort to attend. Youth groups from many churches provided special music. Generally up to 3,000 people attended those meetings.

We observed the phenomenal growth and improvements of the theological training school which Rev. Bokko opened in 1950 to prepare evangelists for his thriving work. The property that was purchased and developed beginning in 1974 became the centre for theological training for the IGF's expansion.

Twenty-four years later the Makale Bible School had high-school-level training courses. They had added college level and theology diploma courses. They had acquired a professor from South Korea who had Oversees Missionary Fellowship (OMF) connections. They had 154 students, some of whom came from other church organizations. The school had well-developed permanent campus buildings and had increased their housing for teachers. Although the district organization still subsidized teachers and staff salaries, students' fees paid for the school's administration and operational expenses. Praise God for this growth in preparing workers for their ever-expanding ministry.

It was at this school site that the IGF commemorated their fiftieth anniversary. What a celebration that was! The IGF leaders emphasised God's victories that blessed them over the years. Youth groups, adorned in uniform outfits, sang well-rehearsed songs. Youth, women, pastors and workers all attended seminars. I enjoyed teaching the women's classes. When Gordon appeared to speak, the clapping welcome response was awesome! They applauded because he had promised the pastors that he would give them a bound copy of his jubilee seminar messages, and because they really enjoyed his solid biblical teaching.

Chorale group performing at the Jubilee Celebration of IGF Church

Despite health problems and other challenges we faced, we cherished the wonderful years of ministry and fellowship with our dear friends of the Indonesian Gospel Fellowship. The mutual benefits of God's blessings were priceless.

Preparing to print the Indonesian *Living New Testament* at Word of Life Publishers in Bandung

CHAPTER 12

WORD OF LIFE PUBLISHERS

When the Indonesia field of The Christian and Missionary Alliance was opened in 1928, it was Dr. Robert A. Jaffray who initiated its beginnings. He established his headquarters in Makassar, a city on the southern tip of the orchid-shaped island in the middle of the archipelago. There he also established a Bible school and a publication ministry. Rev. P.H. Pouw was his capable assistant in the publication department. Since Dr. Jaffray was the son of a newspaper magnate of the *Toronto Globe* in Canada, it was only natural for him to immediately develop a publication department for the needs of his work. That endeavour eventually became known as Penerbit Kalam Hidup (Word of Life Publishers).

In the 1950s both the C&MA field office and the Word of Life Publishers were moved to Bandung in West Java. Though it later proved more convenient to move the C&MA head office to the capital city of Jakarta, Word of Life Publishers stayed in the cooler mountain city of Bandung. They acquired a choice piece of property for an excellent price. The building was near a popular shopping centre in Bandung. Our colleague, Bill Kissell, helped facilitate that transaction.

Some years earlier Word of Life Publishers had become an autonomous department of the GKII national church body. They had elected Sergius M. Udis as its director. Fittingly, Rev. Udis knew Dr. Jaffray, since he graduated from Jaffray Theological School in its early years. He became a faithful voice for both the missionaries and the GKII national church.

In 1974 when Rev. Bud Rudes, the C&MA liaison for the Publishing House, left for his home service he urged Gordon to replace him for a year. It was critical that a dependable liaison be on hand continually, especially since the Indonesian version of *The Living New Testament* was in the final stages of publication. Gordon accepted the assignment.

In the magazine department, two monthly periodicals were published for the Christian community: *Sahabat Gembala* (*The Pastor's Friend*) and the *Kalam Hidup* (*Word of Life*) magazine. At that time Rev. Urbanus Selan and Mr. Soemitro edited, while Mr. Sarojo handled the mailing and clerical duties. They asked for permission to print, in the pastor's magazine, in serial format, Gordon's lesson materials which he had compiled on *The Book of Acts* and my materials on *The Life of Christ*.

By March 2001, subscriber-interest had diminished. The staff was desperate. So Word of Life Publishers' personnel selected four people to go to a magazine publishing seminar in Hong Kong. Donated funds covered their expenses. The seminar provided basic instruction on how to hire staff, evaluate performance, set a budget and cut costs, and how to cope with inflation and economic chaos. The staff immediately set new goals to discover readers' tastes. As a result, both magazines changed format and content, making them more attractive and appealing to subscribers. It was a good start for better magazine production.

Word of Life Publishers provided Bible correspondence courses for interested Christians throughout Indonesia, preparing them for ministry opportunities in their daily lives. For years Rev. Darius Raya managed this work, assisted by Andhi Yhudi.

Mr. Ben Mariva, an East Kalimantan Dyak, had a great ministry in Bandung and in neighbouring areas with the Word of Life Publishers' bookmobile. He did his own stocking and bookkeeping, maintaining a good selection of titles in both the Indonesian and English languages. Word of Life Publishers had its largest display of books in the spacious salesroom in the front of their building, on a main street.

However, about four-fifths of all Word of Life Publishers' books were sold by mail order, going to all parts of Indonesia and to Malaysian Borneo. Gordon helped them develop an excellent billing system to assist their literature distribution. A sizable warehouse at the back of the property provided adequate space for efficient stockpiling of materials. When our grown daughter, Kathleen, came to revisit the country of her birth for several months, she found gainful employment working as an editor of some of their publications.

Other committed Christians came on board to manage the many publication projects. Although the large Indonesian Pertamina Oil Company offered him twice the wage that the Word of Life Publisher's office could pay him, Mr. Yahya Ramali, a well-trained artist, joined the team. Yahya has stayed on staff for many years. He did a superb job of Indonesianizing the cover picture of a translation of Eleanor Doan's *Illustrated Bible Story Book*. This was the first Word of Life Publishers' book to be advertised in Inti Sari, the Indonesian equivalent of *Reader's Digest*. The ad read, "If you love your children, here is a fitting gift for them; only three dollars and seventy-five cents, plus fifty cents postage."

The majority of their publications were printed by offset press, with the typesetting done by a skilled technician on the IBM composer which Bible Literature International donated to Word of Life Publishers. But the most important part of the publishing work was the trained staff of competent translators. Because of competition for employment with foreign companies in the country, there was often a big turnover in translation personnel.

Margaret Gunawan translated *Evolution or Creation*, written by Prof. H. Enoch of Madras, India. That book promised to be in popular demand among the Indonesian academic community. Though most people believed in God as Creator, their schools and colleges taught evolution. When I asked our Jaffray College students about this, they responded indifferently. Through their church affiliation, their own Christian training during their school years had been creation-oriented.

Mr. Ganda Wargasetia was the head translator for the *Gospel Light Sunday School Lessons*. However, his major assignment was the translation of *Firman Allah Yang Hidup*, the Indonesian equivalent of *The Living New Testament*. A reviewing committee did the final editing. The production of this book was managed in cooperation with Living Bibles International. Gordon frequently worked with the translation team, discussing suitable Indonesian equivalents for *The Living Bible* verses under consideration. Though it certainly wasn't his main work, it was his forte, as using his skills in accurately translating from English to Indonesian became his prime interest.

Staff members of Word of Life Publishers, especially from the translation department, received special benefit from a translators' seminar held in Bangkok, Thailand, in 1974. Bible Literature International and Evangelical Literature Overseas were two of the cooperating agencies who shared in its success. Ken McVety, Director of Word of Life Press in Tokyo, organized the seminar. Ken was a former classmate of Gordon's at Canadian Bible College. To meet with him again and to work with him in

155

this extensive assignment was edifying and rewarding. Garth Hunt, former Alliance missionary to Vietnam, also shared in directing the event.

The seminar instructor was Dr. Tom Brewster of Nairobi, Kenya. His vivacious wife, Dr. Betty Sue Brewster, ably assisted him as he lectured from a wheelchair. Along with selected members of Word of Life Publishers staff, Ken McVety had also invited delegates of The Living Bible translation programs from the Philippines, Orissa State in India, Sri Lanka, Thailand, Laos and Cambodia. That was the extensive exposure that Word of Life Publishers translators had with Ken's international team.

As a side benefit for Riani, the Word of Life Publishers' bookkeeper, Ken McVety trained her one-on-one regarding the many details of bookkeeping techniques. She was a keen student and Ken spent many hours beyond the call of duty to teach her.

In The Living New Testament Indonesian translation program, Word of Life Publishers printed test booklets containing the books of Matthew, Ephesians, Titus and Jude in order to get reader reaction. A number of different covers and titles were used to generate feedback. *Sinar Harapan*, in Jakarta, the second largest Christian newspaper in the country, printed the test booklets on their high speed presses. Full-colour covers and inserts, printed in Bandung, were shipped to Jakarta to be added in the binding process.

In June 1975, Christian leaders were introduced to these booklets at a reception for Dr. Kenneth Taylor, who initially prepared *The Living Bible* in English. Mr. Harifa, head of the Protestant division of the Department of Religious Affairs, was an honoured guest at the reception. Ken McVety introduced Dr. Taylor and described the progress of the translation program in some 38 major languages of Asia under his direction.

Dr. Taylor told of God's leading in the development of *The Living Bible*. From its inception it was a simple plan of making family devotions meaningful for his children. Each day on his long commute to and from work, he paraphrased a section of the Bible for his growing family. When Dr. Billy Graham observed how it captivated the minds of many people, he promoted it in his evangelistic meetings, causing it to become a best-seller.

In March 1976, a paperback edition of *Firman Allah Yang Hidup* (*The Living Word of God*) was published with an initial press run of 40,000 copies. In June 1976, a 12,000 copy deluxe edition, with plastic covers and wood-free paper was published.

And in June 1977, a special edition for youth with a "blue jeans" cover became popular. Later, several more editions of 40,000 copies of the original edition were published.

* * * * * * *

A man came to The Word of Life Publishers office asking Gordon for work. Syaaf Syamsuddin, a Muslim from the Minangkabau tribe of Sumatra, had been encouraged by his Christian wife to get a job in a Christian office. Gordon soon realized that what he needed most was to understand how he could become a Christian. Gordon shared specific verses from the Bible with him, explaining the basic steps of receiving Christ as Saviour. Did he understand it? Did he want to receive Jesus as his Saviour? Yes, he did. So Gordon helped him to pray the sinner's prayer, and later he was baptized. But Syaaf still had many things to learn about Christianity. Though he never did get at job at Word of Life Publishers, he did make significant changes in his life.

For me, various counselling and support ministries became routine. The most challenging of all was how our housekeeper was affected by the daily reading of God's Word after her morning work was done. She seemed deeply touched by a testimony in a little booklet I read to her and appeared ready to open her heart to God's truth. At the time I was not aware that the story in that booklet related to the life cycle in her own culture. Its main theme was on heaven, the eternal abode of the saints. I asked her if she believed that the story of Jesus' plan for us in this booklet was true. She said, "Yes." I asked her if she wanted to receive Jesus into her heart. Again, she said "Yes." So right there I led her in the sinner's prayer.

The joy and peace that filled her soul was miraculous. After work, she read the Word avidly in the privacy of her own home. But she wanted the many servants and gardeners, people of her tribe in our vicinity, to receive the same joy she had. And so began a very simple once-a-week Bible study for our housekeeper and her friends.

Some of these people were literate. Some were not. We used an Indonesian translation of a comic-book format of Bible stories. Those who were literate were also assigned to read a verse or two from Scripture. Later I heard that at least one of those servants used that booklet to teach her children the Bible stories. She also took them to a Christmas program in a nearby church.

* * * * * * *

A radio ministry connected with the C&MA national church became a vital project for presenting Christianity to thousands of listeners. Each week a total of 14½ hours of programming were aired twice daily through the *Dawn of Hope* and *Fountain of Love* radio broadcasts for people in Indonesia and Malaysia. The *Fountain of Love* program was on 17 medium-wave stations in Indonesia. Adrian (not his real name), a convert from the majority religion came on staff to answer the listeners' questions. He came to the faith in a very unusual way.

Adrian was a student of mine at Jaffray College. His introduction to Jesus came when he studied comparative religions in high school. He was so captivated by the miraculous powers of the prophet Jesus that he couldn't keep quiet about it. It created great tension and even riots in his school and village. Finally, to keep the peace, his father asked him to leave. Adrian went to Jakarta to get a job.

Amazingly, God put him in touch with a treasured opportunity when his Christian boss invited him to live with them. There, a Bible on a shelf was available for him to read. He read it avidly every day after work. He couldn't understand why his host family never read it except when they went to church on Sundays. Finally, Adrian became a Christian. Later, his company transferred him to work in their upcountry Sulawesi mine site. There he married a Christian girl.

But God still had other plans for Adrian. When he was transferred to work in his company's Makassar office he saw an ad in a paper about Jaffray College. Was this his chance to study the Christian theology? Since his company encouraged staff to take upgrading studies, he took advantage of the opportunity. He took classes at our college in the mornings and worked afternoons to support his family. The story of his conversion to Christianity finally surfaced in the English classes I was teaching. In the last level of English the students had to write a testimony of some special event in their lives. He wrote his conversion story. However, since it was such a sensitive issue, he privately gave me that story and wrote another one to read in class.

Upon graduation from Jaffray College, Adrian became a pastor in a small church in Bandung and helped with the National Church's Christian radio programs. But his major burden was to reach his own people more directly. So he and his wife opened a little shop in a community surrounded by his people. That was the beginning of his first house fellowship. Since then several other house fellowships have been started. He was one of two people from his unreached people group—the largest in the world—who studied at Jaffray College in our time. These difficult ministries cannot be maintained without a consistent, passionate prayer support. The second Jaffray College student from that tribe, named Oce, became a pastor in Bandung.

* * * * * * *

In mid-August 1975, when the Rudes returned to Indonesia after their year of home service, we were able to go back to our work in Toraja, South Sulawesi (Celebes). But our connection with the Word of Life Publishers in Bandung continued, since we were still active in promoting their cause.

A seminar conducted by The Living Bible, International Division, was an exceptional challenge for the IGF brethren in Makale, the capital city of Toraja. The guests who presented the session were Dr. Garth Hunt and his wife Betty from Canada, and Dr. Jake Bellig, pastor of Cathedral at the Crossroads in Castro Valley, California. His wife, Charlotte, was also a member of the team. Rev. Bud Rudes from Word of Life Publishers in Bandung accompanied them for that inaugural seminar. Gordon's first step in preparing for the seminar was to get our old electric generator in Makale functioning again so that a loudspeaker system and screen displays could be used.

Gordon served as translator for Garth Hunt when he spoke to the Makale Bible School student body. When Rev. Rudes addressed the student body in the Indonesian language, Gordon translated the message into English for the Belligs and the Hunts. Later in the day, when Dr. Bellig addressed a reception in the IGF's first church in Makale, Gordon translated his message into the Indonesian language. The IGF brethren ended that festive occasion by providing a banquet for their guests and for all of the IGF delegates who attended the seminar. The Belligs and Hunts spoke of this seminar as their most fascinating ministry in the Far East.

As the guests were returning to Makassar, the two old mission cars they used experienced mechanical problems. Gordon was the designated mechanic to do the roadside repairs, although he could only partially fix the difficulties. Only one vehicle had working headlights, so it had to take the lead. The other car had a major problem with the clutch. At dusk the two cars limped into the city of Makassar. Dr. Bellig and Dr. Hunt were astounded at how Gordon had managed the many mechanical and linguistic needs of the whole day. They were impressed by the breadth of real missionary work.

* * * * * * *

Opening the first Word of Life Publishers bookstore in Jakarta was a momentous occasion. When Bud Rudes gave the introduction at the inauguration celebration of the store, he reported how God's leading had made it possible. The store was strategically located on a main street. The many attractive displays of both Indonesian and English books were a good witness to the purpose of this new facility. At this celebration, Rev. S.M. Udis, Director of Word of Life Publishers in Bandung, had the opportunity to give a few words of testimony. He praised God for the wisdom the Lord had given him during a Bandung Security Police interrogation when the police were contesting the distribution of the Indonesian *Living New Testament*.

The manager of the Jakarta store was Yosafat Maid, an East Borneo Dyak. He left a well-paying job, taking a 50 percent cut in salary so that he could serve the Lord at the bookstore. Attractive and functional bookracks were designed and made by our colleague, Rev. Harold Klassen. The president of the Indonesian national church at that time, Rev. P.G.T. Sallipadang, brought greetings and best wishes to Word of Life Publishers in their new venture. We enjoyed participating in this opening ceremony. Later, a second Word of Life Publishers bookstore opened, making Christian books available to more of the reading public. Part of the second facility housed a wholesale distribution depot.

Word of Life Publishers also placed steel bookracks in secular bookstores. These were maintained by staff who kept the racks filled and picked up the proceeds received from the sales.

The original Word of Life Publishers headquarters in Makassar acquired a strategic corner property on a busy street next to Jaffray College. The property was renovated and opened for the sale of books in August 1977. It was a convenient Bible bookstore for many Christians in the city.

In 1975, Word of Life Publishers, the largest evangelical publisher in Indonesia at the time, gained valuable exposure at a large book fair in Jakarta. Their appealing display exhibited the most popular Christian titles, which included the newly published *Firman Allah Yang Hidup* (*The Living New Testament*), the Indonesian translation of Eleanor Doan's *Illustrated Bible Story Book*, the translation of Don Richardson's *Peace Child* and A.W. Tozer's *The Tozer Pulpit*.

All the larger publishers also presented displays at this fair. BPK Gunung Mulia, the largest Protestant publishing house in Jakarta, had an extensive presentation of their titles. Kanisius, the Catholic publisher, displayed many books relevant to their religious purposes. Petra Jaya, the Pentecostal publisher and the Southern Baptist publishing facility in Bandung, both presented attractive displays. Even major secular publishers such as Gramedia, who printed some Word of Life Publishers' books, displayed large exhibits.

The Indonesian Bible Society, linked to The International Bible Society, revised the Indonesian Bible in 1975. Like the American Bible Society, they made their changes based on a thorough understanding of the linguistic nuances of the Indonesian language. We were fortunate to be able to use that 1975 edition in our Indonesian theological schools.

During this time, Gordon translated Dr. Boyce Blackwelder's *Toward Understanding Romans*. He had it duplicated and bound in paperback for his students at Jaffray College. When his students graduated they were able to also use it as teaching material wherever they served God's people.

How important were good printed materials for helping the Christian community to become strong in faith? Dr. Jaffray would have agreed that they were indispensable. No faith can remain strong for long without the constant reminders of quality printed materials to enable the understanding and boost the fervency of God's children. May God continue to provide excellent reading and study books for His people in Indonesia.

Adina Chapman (front right) on the piano, accompanying singing children at a Jakarta Youth Camp

CHAPTER 13

JAKARTA AND JAVA PROFILES

❦

Our greatest joys in Jakarta and Java were working with and witnessing the ministry of alumni from Jaffray Theological College, Simpson Theological College and other Christian training institutions. These bretheren joined us in our calling of *embracing the mountain.* Actually, our testimony of the work with these colleagues is incomplete, for the full accomplishments in God's Kingdom will only be revealed at the end of time.

* * * * * * *

Our work in Java began when Gordon was introduced to vital contacts in Indonesia's capital, Jakarta, in a September 1978 seminar organized by the General Director of the Office of Religion, Protestant Division. Along with other mission representatives and church leaders, he attended the convention entitled "Functions of Church Leaders to Support the Successful Building of the Nation". Leaders of different organizations shared their concepts with each other and presented their findings to members of the Department of Religion.

We needed The Department of Religion. The department processed many vital business matters of the Mission and the GKII. Sometimes permits were delayed for long periods, or even denied, always involving time-consuming red tape. Crucial to all our work with our churches was understanding and cooperating with this system.

At the Jakarta Bible School we were also asked to fill a gap left by several teachers. The school was directed by Rev. Moses, a pastor of one of the Chinese churches in the city. He paid the scholarships for a small group of Javanese young people from upcountry villages to prepare them for Christian work in their hometowns. These students were required to attend his church every weekend. For some years the C&MA office staff in Jakarta had provided part-time teachers at his request, but they did not participate in the school's administration.

These constraints limited our interaction with their students. Nevertheless, at the school we did have opportunity to provide 500 donated books to their library. Missionary colleagues helped us by making book shelves and typing library cards.

When two of the regular teachers left for studies at the Asian Theological Seminary in Manila, major standard courses weren't taught. And when Judy Gaskin, a C&MA part-time teacher, went on a home service assignment, her vital Christian Education subjects were not covered. Later, teacher Mr. Sumilat, was suddenly called to an assignment in Wamena, Papua New Guinea. Then, in our second year at Jakarta Bible School, about half of the former students were not invited back by Rev. Moses, leaving only a few people in each class.

Ultimately, our C&MA director in the Jakarta office realized that training Java workers in this school was not viable. But for us, God was opening other doors of service. Paul encouraged the church in Colossians, "Whatever you do, work at it with all your heart, as working for the Lord, not for men, since you know that you will receive an inheritance from the Lord as a reward. It is the Lord Christ you are serving." (Colossians 3:23-24)

* * * * * * *

The Word of Life Publishers in Bandung asked Gordon to update the language structure in Rev. Wesley Brill's *Dasar Yang Teguh*—a popular book on basic Christian doctrines. Gordon called this assignment his "escape literature". When a seasoned pastor, one of Gordon's past students, saw him working at it he said, "O, then the doctrine of the book will be changed," for he knew that Gordon's teaching on future prophesies for the church was different from that of the author's. However, preserving the original author's views was an important principle to Gordon as a translator and publisher, so he asked his colleague to proof-read the updated book to ensure that nothing in the original doctrinal emphasis was changed.

During this time Gordon checked over his translations of volume four of Murray Downey's *Book of Books*, a series on the Major Prophets. Mr. Daan Kara, of the Indonesian Department of Education, helped him with the final editing. Because of Mr. Kara's interest in this material, Gordon provided him with the first seven volumes of Murray Downey's books, published by Christian Publications in Pennsylvania. Gordon also proof-read and typeset *The Pioneer*—an annual report of the C&MA missionary work in Indonesia for people in North America who supported our ministries.

I felt God prompting me to rewrite and update my *New Testament Survey* materials I had used over the years. In the introduction I added a brief overview of the history of the 400 silent years between the Old and New Testaments. Then I summarized highlights of each book of the New Testament. My resource materials were:

- *Menggali Isi Alkitab* (*Discovering the Bible*), J. Sidlow Baxter
- *Greek New Testament*, Samuel Baxter & Sons Ltd
- *Penuntun Kedalam Perjanjian Baru* (*Introduction to the New Testament*), Henry H. Halley
- *Matthew Henry's Commentary*, Matthew Henry
- *The Outlined Bible*, Robert Lee
- *The Authority of the Believer*, J.A. MacMillan
- *What the Bible is all About*, Henrietta C. Mears
- *The Wealth, Walk and Warfare of the Christian*, Ruth Paxon
- *Life in the Son*, Robert Shank
- *Search the Scriptures*, Alan M. Stibbs
- *Introduction to the New Testament*, Henry C. Thiessen
- *The Thompson Chain Reference Bible*, Frank C. Thompson
- *Outline Studies in the New Testament*, Wm. Turnbull and E.R. Dunbar

In this adventure, divine guidance spurred me on week after week. My editor was Mr. Niki Nikiyulu, the Overseas Missionary Fellowship's language teacher, who lived across the street from us. Working with him was an excellent writing and language learning experience. Our Word of Life Publishers' artist designed a very attractive cover. First published in 1980, it has become a good seller. Since 1991, this *New Testament Survey* text is required reading in the C&MA national church Bible schools and colleges and most other theological colleges in Indonesia. Many lay people are also edified by it.

Then the delegates of the subsequent field conference re-assigned us to teach at Jaffray College in Makassar. They also asked me to translate *Creative Bible Teaching* by Lawrence Richards—a textbook used for Christian education in our schools.

That was a daunting assignment since translating was not really my gift. Nevertheless, with Rev. John Dana as my editor in Makassar, it proved to be timely. The first five chapters of Lawrence Richard's *Creative Bible Teaching* dealt with contemporary versus conservative theological interpretations of Scripture. At the time, John was attending intensive classes taught by a liberal theologian from Singapore. Suddenly he recognized the conflict between their lecturer's teaching and the basic conservative theology presented in Lawrence Richard's book. It became a vital learning experience for all of the students in that class.

* * * * * * *

Ministry in the GKII churches in Jakarta and throughout Java was a blessed venture. Gordon preached at all of our Jakarta churches at one time or another. I had a weekly teaching ministry with the youth of the Jakarta First GKII church, and taught various ladies' groups in the city. Engaging question and answer classes on the Christian home became a dynamic experience for the ladies at the GKII Tanjong Priok Church. I also taught participants at the quarterly Sunday school teachers' meeting in Jakarta and I enjoyed ministry with the Grogol GKII young people on alternate Sundays. In December it was an honour to be the special speaker at several Sunday school Christmas celebrations.

In June 1980 we had the privilege of taking part in the first annual Jakarta/Java Children and Teens Retreat held in Cipanas. Evangelist Cynthia Chandra provided special messages for the evening services. Gordon and I taught in the youth classes and I played the piano for their worship services.

Over a 2-month period Gordon taught a seminar to approximately 25 GKII church leaders in Surabaya. And later he ministered at an annual GKII Java workers' retreat in Lembang, West Java. At this time in our ministry he was also able to duplicate slides, which missionary colleagues would use during their home assignments.

The culmination of our Jakarta and Java assignment was Gordon's encouraging ministry in May 1980, when he was invited to be the special speaker at the East Borneo, Mahakam District Conference on Sunday mornings and each evening. Simultaneously, the district held a youth camp, where Gordon also preached. There he witnessed evidence of the extensive growth of East Borneo's nine GKII church synods.

* * * * * * *

The primary focus of this Jakarta/Java story is really about how God used the students and alumni from Jaffray College and other C&MA national church Bible schools, who served the Lord in Java. A 1987 Mission field director's report told of eight organized and seven unorganized churches. By the year 2000 there were 72 organized and 42 unorganized churches. How these alumni became Christ's servants in the 114 worship places is detailed in email reports they sent me.

In the chapter "Designated for Victory" some of their stories have already been told. Emails I received in 2001 reported how many ordinary evangelists did extraordinary things as they faithfully served the Lord. Rev. Abraham Lalong and other evangelists have been long-time effective pastors in East Java.

I remember Philipus Gading and his roommate at Jaffray College, who spent days in fasting and prayer to prepare for ministry. That was not a common practice at that time. After graduation Philipus, together with his elders, established the strong Jakasetia church in the Bekasi area of Jakarta. Philipus took further studies at a theological school in Malang, Java. Later, with augmented studies in the United States, he earned his Masters' degree. His courage and his faith are still sustaining him.

Rev. John Mellolo was our student in the Makale Bible School in 1973 to 1974. We called him 'Smiling John' because he exuded such happiness. John and his wife, Damaris, established the Sunter Hijau church in Jakarta, directing it from 1980 to 1989. For the next three years John became the district superintendent of the Jakarta churches. Then he returned to Jaffray College for graduate studies. Back in Jakarta in the year 2000, they were assigned to pastor an older congregation in Tanjong Priok, the port section of Jakarta. Mr. Dasong, one of his most trusted elders, served so well for years in our C&MA Jakarta office.

Rev. Paul Paksoal, another of Gordon's students, was the son of an Indonesian GKII pastor in Papua. He became a Christian in a revival meeting in 1970. Later, when he attended a youth retreat directed by Harold Catto in that province, he felt called to prepare for church ministries. When he finally became a freshman at Jaffray College he was very discouraged. However, his confidence

167

and commitment were strengthened by the example of Nyoman Gama, an upper class student.

Paul observed that Nyoman faithfully followed God in spite of numerous difficulties. Nyoman eventually became the director of a Christian orphanage in Bali that has guided many young people into successful jobs and Christian ministries. Nyoman's wife, Sarah, also a Jaffray College alumna, serves as a pastor in a Balinese church.

After graduation, Paul Paksoal's work led him to assist MAF in Papua. Later he became manager of one of the Jakarta Word of Life Publishers' bookstores. Then he and his wife Priscilla developed a growing GKII national church in the Bekasi area of Jakarta. Simultaneously with that ministry the national church assigned him to raise Foreign Missions Awareness funds in several GKII districts. These resources provided support for Paul and Ari Risamasu, the national church's missionaries in Surinam, South America. Because he had personal humility and received good pastoral mentoring, God continues to bless Paul. More recently Paul and his wife, Priscilla, spent a year in Edmonton, Alberta, Canada, in a church partnership program to learn the principles of nurturing a large congregation.

Paul admired Gordon as a teacher when he watched how tirelessly Gordon worked to achieve big results. When Paul managed the Word of Life Publishers' Bookstore in Jakarta, he was a great promoter of Gordon's translations, especially his eschatology materials. He described Gordon's teaching style as more skilled than that of the professors who had degrees. Gordon, a self-taught man, never acquired a Master's degree.

Erry Agustina seemed like such a modest, unassuming student at Jaffray College. Her story reveals her as anything but ordinary. She called herself a member of a Christian family who didn't really know Jesus as personal Saviour. She was raised by a nominal Catholic uncle who married a Muslim girl. Although Erry went to a Catholic high school for a time, her hungry soul remained unsatisfied.

Then Erry decided that because she couldn't understand the Catholic religion, she would follow the Muslim religion of her aunt. However, her male cousin harassed her every Friday because she didn't attend the mosque worship. Then a friend invited her to attend a Protestant church. But its formal liturgy still left her hungry soul unfulfilled. Finally, a friend from Toraja invited her to attend the First GKII national church in Jakarta. There her long search for peace ended when Erry received Jesus as her personal Saviour on November 10, 1979.

In the joy of her new found faith, spiritual enthusiasm drew her to assist in the work of her church. She promised her Lord that as soon as she had a job she would give 50 percent of her income to support a student at a theological school. At that time, her senior high school was located beside the local cemetery. For Erry, seeing people being buried there almost every day became a wake-up call. By then she was convinced that people who died without knowing Jesus had no hope of eternal life. Her final step of surrender came at a GKII youth retreat in Kaliurang, Yogyakarta, Java, where she committed her life to God for service.

That is what finally brought her to Jaffray College in Makassar. Her primary goal was to understand the Bible so she could confidently teach it to other people. She admired her teachers who taught with integrity and lived exemplary lives in their service for God and she longed to develop an intimate fellowship with her Lord. Erry wanted to grasp Christ's burden for the lost, to serve people no matter how lowly their social status.

Why was Erry burdened for the poor who earned less than a survival income? She cared because Jesus loved them, because people generally ignored them and because of Dr. A.B. Simpson's example in caring for the poor. Her third church planting in Rawa Kalong (meaning swamp land) was made up of people from the poorest of the poor—pedicab drivers and garbage pickers. Because one person experienced miraculous healing, they were very ready to hear God's Word and 27 people accepted Christ as Saviour. In October 1999 she baptized the first four families and dedicated their children to the Lord.

Since graduating from Jaffray College in 1987 with a Bachelor of Religious Education degree, Erry has served her Lord with a passion for the lost. At the start she became an assistant to the pastor at the GKII first church in Jakarta. Then in June 1988 she became pastor of the GKII El Shaddai Fellowship in Bekasi. In May 1991 she planted a church in the Wisma Jaya area, which is now served by Evangelist Lenny S. In July 1995 Erry started a new church in Tangerang, Jakarta. In September 1998 she began the work at Rawa Kalong, Jakarta, where she still serves at the time of this writing. Her assistant is an internship student from Simpson Theological College in Ungaran, Central Java. With help from Jakarta churches and missionary friends, Evangelist Erry has provided social assistance for poor families and food for underfed children. She is one more example of Jaffray College alumni, who, together with colleagues from other C&MA schools, are *embracing the mountain* for God's Kingdom in Java.

Ivone Palar was first taken to church by her mother when she was still very young. She remembers a song her Sunday school teacher taught her saying "sweet children go to heaven and bad children go to hell". As a result, by doing good works she worked hard at being a "sweet child". When she was 14 years old, a friend invited her to a Vacation Bible School held at a GKII national church in Jakarta. When her teacher emphasized Ephesians 2:8-9, she was smitten with the thought that her good works couldn't save her. She received Jesus' forgiveness when she realized that He had died for her sins. It changed her life. She became hungry and thirsty for God's word and was strengthened in her faith when Pastor Rev. Khristyanto counselled her.

Hearing the story of William Carey, missionary to India, Ivone wondered—could she become God's servant too? In her searching mind, with lessons taught by Rev. Gordon Swenson at the Kelapa Gading Church and later at a youth retreat in Central Java, she began to seriously consider serving God. She attended Judy Gaskin's training classes, received a certificate and started teaching Sunday school. While attending Margaret and Vernon Neigenfind's classes on principles of teaching, she also learned how to prepare Bible lessons.

Ivone's decisive moment came when she attended a youth retreat the second time. Sarce Urias, a Jaffray College internship student, guided Ivone through her spiritual battles. Her father was her strongest opponent, saying, "There is no future in becoming God's servant." In a youth retreat the following year Rev. John Dana, the special speaker, talked about Isaiah 6:8, "Here I am, send me." It captured Ivone's heart and she could no longer hold back. In a vision she saw dying souls facing eternal judgement. She went to the altar and surrendered her life to God. Soon after that, Ivone and her friend, Erry Agustina, were on their way to Jaffray Theological College.

Characteristically, Ivone started her Christian life on the run while she was still young. As her mentor, Judy Gaskin, the southern United States missionary lady, would say, "she ain't stopped runnin' yet". Several study trips with Judy to Singapore and to the United States have added immense insight and experience to Ivone's ministry at youth camps. In 1996, Big

Sandy Camp in Minnesota adopted their Java Good News Youth Camp as a partner ministry. Under Judy's direction, money came to build the camp at a site surrounded by people of the local majority religion. Since then they have also received revenue when other church groups rent their facility. For eight years they have used this camp for children and young people's camps and for church leaders' seminars.

When the Youth Camp was confronted with conflicts from their contentious neighbourhood in 1999, their programs had to be cancelled. They watched their facility day and night because rumours spread that they would be attacked. Many problems were tactfully resolved. During that year the camp committee taught groups of children in different areas of Jakarta.

Thankfully, in the year 2000, camps resumed with 18 teachers ministering to 600 campers. They studied the fourfold gospel, and were also given lessons on the harmful use of drugs—a rampant problem among youth in metropolitan areas. Besides regular classes, they also hold Bible quizzes and competitions for singing groups. For years this camp has challenged hundreds of young people to commit their lives to Christ. In 2001, Ivone Palar was chosen by the Indonesian GKII National Organization to be Director of Youth and Children's Ministries. Their camp staff are some of the many workers who participate in the work for God's Kingdom in Java.

* * * * * * *

This chapter on the Lord's work in Java would not be complete without mentioning the ministry of the Simpson Theological College (STTS). In 1983 the college had a simple beginning in the city of Semarang. By 1985 they were able to move to their new campus in Ungaran, near Semarang in Central Java. C&MA missionaries have always assisted in teaching. At least seven members of the teachers and leaders at STTS were Jaffray College alumni.

Rev. Marso Daniel, Director of STTS from 1991 to 2001, sent a report of the struggles and victories in his life. As the son of a faithful pastor in East Borneo, he considered himself a good person. Though he memorized many Scripture verses, his infractions brought much hardship to his parents. Eventually their GKII synod disciplined the parents for not correcting their son, which was a hard lesson for Marso also.

After receiving Christ as Saviour his whole life changed. His father's nightly Bible reading and prayer times with his family were his prime examples of faithful Christian living. Marso learned practical lessons by watching his father pray for the sick and observing his patient dealing with willful church members. Most memorable were his father's intense deliverance prayers that freed people from the control of evil spirit powers. This left a great impression on Marso.

During his student days at The Willfinger Theological School in the Krayan, East Borneo, and later at Jaffray College in Makassar, Marso led Bible study groups, singing groups and worship services—all excellent learning experiences. At Jaffray College, being disciplined for disobeying school rules and sometimes failing academically were also valuable lessons.

After graduation Marso taught at the Jaffray Theological Institute in Jakarta for a short period, and became pastor of the East Jatinegara GKII church for a year. For another three years he was pastor of the Sunter Hijau Church in north Jakarta. Then the district synod assigned him to be Director of Simpson Theological College in Ungaran, Central Java. He said that in his ten years at the school, his greatest reward was seeing his students become Christ's faithful servants who were prepared by the Spirit of God for ministry. His major concern was to reach people in Java for Christ. In 2001, Marso was elected to be the secretary for Dr. Yakob Tomatala—the new President of the GKII national church. He continues teaching Christian leaders in upgrading seminars to this day.

His wife, Betty Elysabeth Anthon, daughter of Pastor Anthon Ranying in West Borneo, said that her strongest incentive for ministry came from her parents' faithful service in their church work. She became a Christian when she heard a lady sing the song, "Let the Lower Lights Be Burning" (P.P. Bliss). In May that same year, through a dream and through her parents' prayer for her, she felt a call to give her life to God for full-time service. Until morning, she read over and over, "'Come out from them and be separate, says the Lord' … 'I will be a Father to you and you will be my sons and daughters,' says the Lord Almighty." (II Corinthians 6:17a, 18) She was especially challenged to be faithful to God through Gordon's lessons on the books of Daniel and Revelation.

In her studying at the Immanuel Bible School in West Borneo and at Jaffray Theological College, Betty was confronted with school rules. She matured with the discipline of her teachers and the advice of fellow students. Two Scripture verses that helped her to overcome her struggles were Philippians 4:13, "I can do everything through him who gives me strength." and I Thessalonians 5:24, "The one who calls you is faithful and he will do it." After graduating she married Marso Daniel and worked with him in East Borneo, in Jakarta, at Simpson Theological College, in Ungaran, Central Java and later in Jakarta.

In her work in Java she was most encouraged when people became Christians through cell group Bible studies and when her students faithfully served the Lord. The integrity of her teachers during her student days had been the best Christian example for her ministry.

In November 2001 the National GKII Assembly elected Dr. Ruth Selan as the new Director of Simpson Theological College. Her basic challenges are: to develop extension classes in East and Central Java; and to establish majors in Theology, in Contextual Ministries and in Christian Education at the college—a daunting job.

Students and faculty from STTS travel to district churches every other week to create new student interest and to encourage positive interaction between the school and the churches. The Kingdom of God will keep growing as His servants stand together with one heart and mind for the Lord in Java.

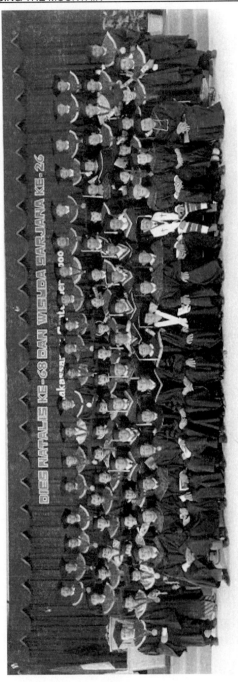

Professors and graduating class of 2000, Jaffray Theological College (STTJ)

CHAPTER 14

<u>DIVERSITY IN MINISTRY</u>

In writing to the Colossians, Paul made the compelling statement, " … God has chosen to make known among the Gentiles the glorious riches of this mystery, which is Christ in you, the hope of glory." (Colossians 1:27) Jesus Himself promised the power for that hope, "But the Counselor, the Holy Spirit, whom the Father will send in my name, will teach you all things and will remind you of everything I have said to you." (John 14:26) Praise God, through His Spirit, Christ would always be there for us.

* * * * * * *

We had to trust God to prepare us for the diverse challenges we would face as we returned to Jaffray Theological College in Makassar in 1980. It was reported that there were many different people groups represented and students from 20 different church organizations attended the college. Although each spoke their own dialect, our common language of communication was the official Indonesian language.

I was assigned the daunting job of coordinating English as a Second Language (ESL) courses at the College. Amazingly, even before I started, God provided a Summer Institute of Linguistics staff member from the local university to teach me a crash course in the principles of teaching ESL. Because the course was functional and easy to use, it relieved me of many hours of preparation for my classes. In time, and with some assistance, we taught six levels of English—levels one and three in one semester and two and four in the next, later adding the higher levels. I also had the privilege of tutoring at least four people with intensive ESL courses, preparing them for studies and experiences abroad. An added blessing for me was teaching the New Testament Survey course.

Gordon's delight in the classroom was teaching many eager young people. Generally, in Indonesian colleges, lessons were merely received as dictated. In Gordon's classes discussions with the keenest students became the norm. One of the students who enjoyed the discussions most later became a professor at Jaffray College.

On one occasion, three seasoned pastors, who were Gordon's friends, decided to take one of his courses. When one of them felt reluctant to raise a certain question, he whispered to a younger student of their tribe, urging him to pose the point. After providing a good answer Gordon looked at the seasoned pastor and said, "Now that we've answered Rev. Sallipadang's question, let's get on with the lesson." The class roared with laughter!

Preparing famous theologians' translated lesson materials presented a continuing challenge for my husband. As soon as Gordon completed one set of class materials, he would be assigned a new course with no available teaching materials. But this was a welcomed opportunity. He enjoyed working in the field of linguistics most of all.

* * * * * * *

Almost every weekend we had diverse opportunities for ministry. Churches in the city that had connections with Jaffray College frequently requested a Sunday morning guest speaker— often a missionary. And when December came, various groups of Christian office workers and people from specific tribal groups requested devotional messages for their Christmas events. These requests came in addition to providing seasonal messages for church youth groups, ladies fellowship meetings and Sunday school programs. Christmas celebrations continued for weeks. Year-round we and our missionary colleagues took turns leading the English Christian Worship services in the city. Once I was given an opportunity to speak to nursing students in an initiation ceremony.

Meanwhile, having a burden to reach other than Christian young people in the city, I started a weekly evening class, using the Bible as a base for English conversation. The session always ended in prayer. For one of those students it became a life-changing experience.

Although Abigail Palinggi regularly taught the young people in her church, spiritually she felt empty and hungered for more.

Friends belonging to a cult began sharing their religion. Her pastors warned her not to follow their teaching. When she asked them why, they could never give a definitive answer. Eventually she stopped teaching at her church and read everything the cult members gave her. Later, when asked what originally attracted her to their religion, she responded by saying that she was disillusioned with nominal Christianity and was looking for something better. "What's more," she said, "they cared about me."

Then Abigail's brother sponsored her at an Inter-Varsity Fellowship camp in Java. When I saw her at an English Worship Service in Makassar, she had just returned. She approached me saying, "I have Jesus in my heart and it's so wonderful!" I replied, "Come and tell me about it."

For a whole week she had battled against the powers of darkness that were seeking to destroy her. Friends prayed for her intensely. The last day she finally gave her problems over to God and was gloriously liberated. On the eve of her departure from Jakarta she was again attacked with paralyzing fears. She feared that the cult members, who had influenced her for eight years, would try to contact her again when she returned. Her sister-in-law, a dear Christian, prayed with her until she found release in Jesus.

I spent several weeks counselling Abigail one-on-one. Together, we studied Scripture verses that would sustain her against future deceptions. She embraced me with tears of gratitude, recording in her notebook every precious lesson she received. Wanting her friends to receive the same joy she had, she brought them to be counselled with and prayed for too.

Many months later, after I taught her intensive ESL classes, she was able to study at the Asian Theological Seminary in Manila. Upon returning to her job in Makassar she became a vibrant voice for God's Kingdom, establishing many Bible study groups for college and high school students. Several times a year she organized large rallies where a special speaker helped these young people seal their commitment to Christ. Praise God for Abigail's faithfulness to her Lord. Eventually she married a Christian widower and moved to another city where she serves God as opportunities come.

* * * * * * *

Gordon's obligation as member of the C&MA Executive Board provided an extra blessing when Paul Paksoal, one of our alumni, asked him to conduct a seminar on eschatology. As a result, after the board meetings were completed, he spent two days teaching three-hour sessions to Jaffray College alumni who were Indonesian GKII pastors in Jakarta churches and to students from Jaffray College's extension classes in Jakarta. Everybody was grateful for the edifying lessons on one of Gordon's favourite subjects.

In 1984 the Makassar Jaffray College School Board asked Gordon to be an advisor to their library staff. This added another major assignment—transferring all the library books from an old, pre-World War II building to a new administration building. With the help of a fellow missionary, they installed new steel shelves in the library. Then in a one-day move, with students assisting, all the library books were transferred to the new facility and Mrs. Ribka Kurang began working as the librarian. Gordon and I both spent a great deal of time putting a card catalog in order to better facilitate the loaning of books.

Gordon and Adina Chapman, c. 1978

On May 24, 1984, seventeen Jaffray College students were set apart for internship ministries. Most of them were assigned to do church planting in Java. Some worked in Bandung and Jakarta, while others reached out to people in other towns in West, Central and East Java. Several Jaffray College alumni asked to join them. Though a few faced severe opposition, one student asked to stay with a family of the majority religion. Reluctantly the family received him for several weeks. The Lord so blessed his loving attitude and his faithful witness that the father in the home soon put his faith in Christ. Other family members followed. The father even offered to provide transportation on his motorbike to assist in ministry opportunities.

Quite a few students organized new groups of believers which they mentored in the Christian faith. Others taught religion in elementary and junior high schools. Through these children our Jaffray College students made vital contacts with families. In his assigned area, one student organized the showing of the film "*Jesus of Nazareth*" and began several Bible study groups. There, about 50 people asked for baptism. Concerned about what would happen to them when that student returned to college in January, the people asked, "Can't he stay to teach us?" Great was their hunger to know more about God's Word.

In September 1985 Rev. Peter Anggu's hopes to study for a Doctor of Ministries degree at Fuller Theological Seminary in Pasadena, California, finally materialized. His wife and two of his children accompanied him. Meanwhile, Mr. Gideon Tandirerung and Rev. Sadrak Kurang, with his family, returned from studies in Manila and began teaching at Jaffray College. Rev. John Dana, an excellent teacher, felt the need to move to Jakarta where he became Director of the Good News Organization, as well as administrator of their training school. For a time he also assisted in STTJ's extension classes in Jakarta. Jaffray College also had extension courses in Tana Toraja, in Bali, and for a while assigned people to teach foreign workers at a plant in Balik Papan, East Borneo.

Meanwhile, our greatest goals for Jaffray College were to strengthen the spiritual atmosphere by having more classes in the study of the God's Word and to emphasize the vital ministry of the Holy Spirit. How did Jaffray College alumni emerge in this context? During 1997 to 1999 I received many encouraging emails confirming their faithfulness in service.

Since we received students from 20 different organizations, friends in Canada sometimes asked us what percentage became workers in the GKII national church. Actually, a majority of the students became pastors, district leaders or teachers in the 29 GKII theological schools which the national church had throughout Indonesia by then.

Rev. Lolly Dungau became Director of the Tenggarong Theological College in East Borneo. A missionary colleague spoke of him as a man of integrity, an effective preacher and a godly family man. Of Gordon's teaching Lolly said: "I appreciated the way you had mastered general knowledge as well as scriptural truth. A special blessing for me was the three semesters of Theology I took, and the courses on Daniel/Revelation, Major Prophets, Apologetics and Christian Ethics. May everything you taught us be shared by your students throughout Indonesia. Your friendly attitude in and out of the classroom was a great example to me."

The Tenggarong Theological College elected Rev. Yoel Lufung as Academic Dean of their school. Besides being a teacher, the college also appointed him to be Treasurer of the Board of their building program. Rev. Lufung is pleased about the school's activities in evangelistic outreach as a program for upgrading the status of their community. Because they functioned under the arm of the government's Public Service Unit, they had more freedom in teaching God's Word. Yoel Lufung is also concerned for Christians who are being persecuted in various provinces of Indonesia.

The East Borneo GKII national church district contains a large community of Christians. Rev. Elly Djuk, one of the Jaffray College alumni who were directors of their nine synods in the year 2000, sent me a report of God's leading in his life. Although his first assignment after graduation was teaching at the Tenggarong Theological College for several years, he was later elected as leader of one of the synods.

As a young married man, Elly had had a major question: Why should he become a Christian? At the time his father was very ill. He vowed that if Jesus would heal his father he would believe in Him. If not, he would not become a Christian. When a pastor prayed for his father he was instantly healed, and Elly followed through on his vow. The pastor was pleased to lead Elly and his wife in prayer as they accepted Jesus as Saviour.

Actually, as a third grade student, Elly had a passionate desire. He wanted to attend Jaffray College, so that he could be like Rev. Usat Sigau, the pastor in his church, who was such an amiable person. After finishing elementary school in his area, he attended junior and senior high school studies at the Long Bia

Bible School in East Borneo. Then he was eligible to study at Jaffray College in Makassar. There, he often did not have enough money to buy food for several days. Nevertheless, he committed himself to be willing to suffer if necessary. He believed that if God helped other students to endure hardship, surely He would help him too and in the process he would become a stronger servant for the Lord.

Elly appreciated the examples of his teachers at Jaffray College. He admired Gordon for always being well prepared for his classes and he enjoyed his teaching style. Elly perceived us as being very disciplined and patient, and was genuinely affected by our good husband/wife relationship.

Rev. Elly Djuk said that his most fulfilling efforts in ministry were solving peoples' problems and counseling couples to be reconciled when they were on the verge of divorce. When people received Jesus as Saviour, he was genuinely blessed because they were guided by the power of the Holy Spirit. To Pastor Elly, the Holy Spirit's work in peoples' lives was God's miracle. He observed that the more his parishioners participated in prayer for the Spirit's intervention, the greater the blessings in his whole congregation. These were his greatest rewards.

Ludi Lian, in his written testimony for his sixth level of ESL at Jaffray College, shared an interesting event from his childhood. When Ludi was very ill, his parents were ready to take him to the witch doctor because they had no other hope for his survival. Though Ludi wasn't yet a teenager he'd had enough experience in Sunday school to know that there was a better way. He begged his parents to take him to their pastor instead. God honored Ludi's faith. When the pastor prayed for him he was healed. This event led him to prepare for the Lord's service at Jaffray College in Makassar.

Rev. Leo Sumule sent me an interesting email telling of God's direction in his life. His parents' genuine Christian faith had a profound influence on him. They led him in prayer to receive Christ as Saviour. Then, while attending special meetings at 16 years of age, he felt God calling him to serve Him the rest of his life.

At Jaffray College Leo thanked God for how his teachers exemplified the Christian life. What encouraged him so much was their humility and their faithfulness in service. Special counseling from several of them helped strengthen his faith. When he returned to Samarinda in East Borneo he became a teacher at the

Tenggarong Theological College. He became involved in Christian youth activities, providing them with Bible study materials and promoting good fellowship.

Leo praised God for the contribution of excellent teaching materials that Gordon and I provided for the students at Jaffray College. To him they are essential for his work as a teacher in East Borneo. He admitted that he still impersonates some of Gordon's teaching habits. Gordon used to say: "I teach you to 'ganggu' you" (literally meaning to challenge you). If his students slipped into class late he would say as a pun: "Selambat pagi" (you're late), instead of "Selamat pagi" (good morning).

Leo remembered a special chapel message Gordon gave after having been diagnosed with terminal cancer. Students questioned why this should happen to him. My husband's answer was: "Why not me?" Gordon believed that Christians are not necessarily exempt from suffering and illness.

Later Leo was given a scholarship to earn his Masters' degree at Wheaton College in Illinois. There he met Stephanie who later became his wife. When he graduated in 1996 his wife joined him as he returned to Samarinda to resume his teaching. In 2001, the GKII National Church Conference elected Leo as National Youth Director. One of his five-year goals was to see every young Christian identify with Christ as recorded in Philippians 3:10, "I want to know Christ and the power of his resurrection and the fellowship of sharing in his sufferings ..." He purposed to visit every district to strengthen their leadership and to advise them on making plans for annual youth retreats.

Leo had momentous ministries when he took a team of students to a far interior village in East Borneo. He once called this location the "University of Witchcraft" since witch doctors from the whole area would go there for training in satanic powers. In one village it was frightening to see a 32 year-old woman living in a cage because she was possessed by demons and could not be controlled. Leo's team engaged in intense prayer warfare, claiming the liberating power of Jesus to release her from bondage. Praise God, she was freed from 16 years of demon-possession. This deliverance created a breakthrough for Christianity in the district. Even some shaman, seeing what the power of God could do, gave up their witchcraft and became followers of Christ. It had a profound effect on the whole area.

But Satan does not relinquish his grip without a fight. Several weeks later when the team revisited the village, Ani, the liberated lady's sister, came running after the evangelist with a knife determined to kill him. Some of the team members were able to get the knife away from her. The team prayed and fasted all night, crying to God for Ani's deliverance also. On a later trip more villagers became followers of Christ. When 800 new believers urgently needed good instructions in the Christian faith, theology students were dispatched to serve them on a regular basis. Leo said that a strong prayer-support system would be the only thing that could liberate these people from their bondage. If friends prayed for them in the power of Jesus name, deliverance would come.

Several years later, there was further evidence that the evil one does not submit willingly. When three missionaries on staff at the Tenggarong Theological College experienced severe back pain, they flew to Singapore for medical help. How was it possible that three missionaries and some Indonesian staff were all afflicted at once?

Then Leo reported excitedly, "You'll never believe what's happening here! Revival has come to our campus. Since Friday we have met for prayer every evening. Prayers often last until the early morning hours. Students are confessing their sins. There is a freedom in worship we have never experienced before." Pursuing holiness and unity were the key components of this victory.

The previous week several senior students were discipling a female freshman. When they came to an impasse, they took her to a professor. He sensed a demonic presence and called the students to a special prayer time. As they gathered, they felt compelled to confess their own sins first. Then the outpouring of the Holy Spirit began.

Sin was exposed when that female freshman confessed that she had been sent by a witch doctor from a northern village in East Borneo. Her assignment was to destroy female students by gaining control over them, convincing them to wear bracelets that would bind them to her and her master. As the students prayed into the night they repented of their own sins, and then prayed for this freshman's deliverance until freedom came to her.

Two nights later, another female freshman explained that she had been sent by another witch doctor. Her assignment was to destroy the professors at Tenggarong Theological College. Then she was to move on, spending a year at each of the other Indonesian GKII colleges to do likewise. Once again professors and students prayed intensely until this second witch doctor's emissary was also liberated from her bondage of darkness. These two former agents of Satan had been bitter enemies. In a final confirmation of their victory, they came together to prove their deliverance by showing God's love for each other.

Victory also came to people at the Tenggarong Theological College because Christ is ever interceding for us at the right hand of the Father, as is written in Hebrews 7:24-25, "but because Jesus lives forever, he is a permanent priesthood. Therefore he is able to save completely those who come to God through him, because he always lives to intercede for them." And in Romans 8:34, "... Christ Jesus, who died—more than that, who was raised to life—is at the right hand of God and is also interceding for us."

Jesus' prayer for his disciples in John 17:9-11 is another source of divine strength. He said: "I pray for them. ... for those you have given me, for they are yours. ... Holy Father, protect them by the power of your name—the name you gave me—so that they may be one as we are one." The unity Jesus spoke of was crucial. Students and staff at the Tenggarong Theological College realized that without unity the delivering power of the Spirit could not come. Praise God that as Christians obeyed, there was power in Jesus, the victorious Lord.

On February 9, 2002, Leo reported on how their second semester started with the first eight-hour fasting and prayer session at their college in almost six years. Beginning with praise, it soon became an important confession and repentance time. They prayed for their local evangelism program and for global evangelism, and ended with a healing service. With 360 students at their college, they were frequently confronted with discipling needs. As a result, while Leo was away for ten days on a ministry tour, Leo's wife, Stephanie, organized student prayer groups and got the National Youth Ministries program on track. It was a difficult time for them. How they needed the support of faithful prayer warriors.

* * * * * * *

In May 1986 Rev. Sadrak Kurang, Rev. Ruben Chung Lim and four other team members were assigned to go on an evangelistic trip to Sarawak, in Malaysian Borneo. This would be a new experience for Sarawak churches. The team requested passports from the Indonesian Immigration Office but they were denied. At Jaffray College much prayer went up to the throne of

God. In the end, the Immigration Office issued, not passports but travel documents. In Sarawak, sixteen churches enthusiastically received the group. Young people from the neighboring country of Brunei, where Protestants did not have religious freedom, followed the team around in their travels. The team conducted Christian Education seminars, organized youth camps and preached in military camps. During that period 1,022 people prayed for salvation or renewal. Many people asked for prayer for healing and many surrendered their lives to God for service. This outreach demonstrated Jaffray College's excellent connection with Christians in a neighboring country.

Many students from Malaysian Borneo came to study at Jaffray College. When they finished their studies they became pastors, district leaders and teachers in the theological school in Malaysia. Having a common language with Indonesia was a big asset. In fact, Malaysian young people would often cross the border to attend youth camps in Indonesian East Borneo. Gordon's many translated books, as well as the resource materials from the Word of Life Publishers in Bandung, Java, provided a tremendous help for the church's ministry in Malaysian Borneo. The use of *Nyanyian Kemenagnan Iman* (*Songs of Victorious Faith*), a popular hymn book for many Protestant denominations in Indonesia, published by Word of Life, revolutionized their worship services.

* * * * * * *

In 1986 Gordon suddenly faced an unbelievable medical crisis. For years he had suffered severe back pains. In our early days in Borneo, stooping over engines to repair them became very difficult. In the 1960s, when a physician took X-Rays of his back he said Gordon had the backbone of a 90 year-old man. By early November 1986, arthritic back pains became so critical that sitting was almost impossible. However, he felt he had to fulfill his promise to preach at the Latimojong Indonesian Gospel Fellowship Church. Afraid to sit down—he walked back and forth in the pastors' prayer room as he waited for his turn on the platform. Appearing at the podium, he preached passionately about the Christian life, especially using Dr. Robert Jaffray's sacrificial service as an illustration.

Before long, Gordon was confined to bed. If he lay flat on his back he experienced only a limited amount of pain. Standing was possible but getting into a standing position was excruciatingly difficult. I managed to get him to a doctor, but getting into a car caused agonizing pain. In the doctor's office, when sharp pains hit him hard he turned white as a sheet and broke out into a cold sweat.

When the doctor ordered X-Rays I had to figure out a way to get him to the X-Ray office. Using a camp-cot canvas, I devised a way to make a stretcher by inserting bamboo poles into its side slots. With this stretcher our students were able to carry him, moving him from his bed onto the floor of their pickup truck. At the X-Ray office they carefully moved him from the stretcher onto the X-Ray table. The lumbar region showed damage.

Dr. Santosa, the best surgeon in Makassar, together with his neurologist friend came to our home to see Gordon. They decided that his best option was to see an orthopedic surgeon in Singapore. They provided hypodermic pain-killers for his trips to Jakarta and Singapore. At the Mt. Elizabeth Hospital in Singapore, a CT scan and a lumbar mylogram showed extensive osteo-arthritis the length of Gordon's spine. However, the orthopedic surgeon was not ready to operate. After ten days of traction with deep-heat therapy, there was some improvement but not enough to warrant our return to Makassar.

Spending the next several days in a Singapore hotel proved that returning to Makassar would be a problem. When we phoned our Field Director in Jakarta, he said, "Don't return to Indonesia! Go directly to Canada!" Gordon was devastated. The surgical correction he had hoped to get in Singapore didn't happen. But God had a better plan. A former missionary colleague in Singapore invited us to stay in her home. She had business connections that enabled us to phone our families in Canada. She also made the best travel arrangements for us. Her company was later reimbursed by our C&MA organization.

We arrived in Edmonton, Canada, in mid-December, 1986. While searching out further medical aid nearby, we stayed with our daughter and her husband, Kathleen and Dale Ibsen, in Stettler, Alberta. For an added blessing, other family members also joined us there for a warm Christmas celebration. Our son-in-law, Dale, could only get an appointment several weeks later to see Dr. Thiessen in Calgary, who then referred Gordon to Dr. Thomas, an excellent neurosurgeon.

Another mylogram and CT scan at the Calgary Rockyview General Hospital showed a significant narrowing of the nerve channel at the L1-L2 level of the lumbar region. I was with Gordon in his hospital room when the surgeon gave us his verdict. He said the surgery would be very critical. It might paralyze him from the waist down for the rest of his life, or it could eventually free him from pain. What did Gordon choose to do? We asked if we could speak to our family physician before we made our decision.

When Dr. Thiessen arrived the next morning we asked what hope there was to return to Indonesia by merely depending on anti-inflammatory medication. He said that without surgery it would not be wise to return. Since returning to the field was a priority, we felt that we had to trust God for the best surgical outcome. Dr. Thomas was pleased, saying it was the right choice. I notified our children of the surgery which was scheduled for February 10. Our oldest son, Ken, who was on a work assignment in Saudi Arabia at the time, received a compassionate leave to join us in Calgary. His presence was very comforting for me.

The doctor opened Gordon's spinal column at the affected area. He carefully eased the spinal cord out of the way and removed all the offending arthritic spurs that had caused him so much pain. The surgery went well. He was in the recovery room for a time, and when he returned to his hospital ward in great spirits, we were there to greet him.

Physiotherapists showed him how to safely sit up and move around. By the next morning he was ordered to get on his feet. He was assigned special high-step walking exercises. When people passed him in the hallway, Gordon joked about the "deep snow" around him. He couldn't have been happier! Subsequently, more advanced exercises helped him regain his strength. By May 1987 he was able to join Dale, Kathleen and me as we traveled to our C&MA Annual Council in the United States. In mid-August we arrived back in Jakarta, Indonesia. Our sovereign God had miraculously renewed Gordon's health and prepared him for another wonderful term of service.

Gordon Chapman prays during graduation ceremonies
at Jaffray Theological College

CHAPTER 15

A GOD-ORDAINED FINALE

There is triumph in the finale if God is in it. Philippians 1:6 strengthened our faith, "being confident of this, that he who began a good work in you will carry it on to completion until the day of Christ Jesus." And Psalm 77:14-15 assured us that God had power to do it, "You are the God who performs miracles; you display your power among the peoples. With your mighty arm you redeemed your peoples." God would display His power again in our final years. During our last home service time in Canada in 1986 we had frequently asked our church friends to pray for God's intervention in four crucial areas:

- The choice of the next president for the GKII national church
- The choice of president for Jaffray Theological College
- The choice of director for Word of Life Publishers
- Our appointment as we returned to Indonesia for our final term of service

Coming back from our home service leave in Canada, we arrived in Jakarta to hear that August 23-30, 1987, had been set aside for the All-Indonesia National Church Conference. It was scheduled to be held at Ciburu, just outside of the Jakarta city limits. The Mission's Executive Committee members, including Gordon, were invited to attend as observers.

At a rather lengthy official opening, the Indonesian Minister of Religious Affairs and the Director General of the Christian Department of the Ministry of Religious Affairs submitted their greetings. Then Dr. Anggu, the keynote speaker, stressed the need for the National Church to truly become a missionary organization, lest they end up being ingrown and self-serving. He said that living the life of Christ on a daily basis would be *sine qua non*—that without which—the organization could not become what God intended it to be. The opening ceremony was televised in Jakarta the next day.

Guest speaker, Dr. Rodrigo Tano, Director of the Alliance Biblical Seminary in Manila, Philippines, effectively used Ephesians 4 in three sermons during the conference to encourage the brethren to faithfully serve God in unity and love. Rev. Sergius M. Udis, retiring Director of Word of Life Publishers, suffered a stroke early on in the conference. He was pronounced dead on arrival at the hospital—a sobering moment.

The conference delegates became apprehensive when they learned of some of the nominations and the rules that had been laid out for elections. Things were simmering that weren't ethical or Christ-like. How would God answer the prayers of His people?

The nominating committee had selected Dr. Peter Anggu as candidate for National Church President. However, he had just earned his Doctor of Ministries degree on a C&MA mission scholarship at Fuller Theological Seminary for the purpose of his return to Jaffray College as President. Despite their persistence, he insisted several times to the committee that he didn't feel gifted for the National Church office and withdrew his name. Dr. Anggu recognized that his gifts were in teaching.

Our hope lay in a prophetic word that had been clearly spoken in Isaiah 14:24, "The Lord Almighty has sworn, 'Surely, as I have planned, so it will be, and as I have purposed, so it will stand.'" After lengthy heated debates, the National Church Executive Committee members, who were all alumni from Jaffray College, changed the rules to allow nominations from the floor. Then elections were held. When I later heard of the results I could hardly believe that God had directed such decisive miracles. Man had delegated, but God had determined the outcome. A famous adage—"The best-laid plans of mice and men ... " was apropos:

To a Mouse
But, mousie, thou art not thy lane,
In proving foresight may be vain;
The best-laid schemes o' mice an' men
Gang aft agley,
An' lea'e us naught but grief an' pain,
For promis'd joy!
—Robert Burns

These were the election results that called for a victory song:

- Rev. Matias Abai was re-elected as President of the Indonesian National Church.
- Dr. Peter Anggu was returned to his position as President of Jaffray College.
- Mr. Soemitro was elected to be Director of Word of Life Publishers.
- The conference delegates declared that Gordon's expertise as lecturer at Jaffray Theological College be maintained.

Though we had been fearful of what our final four years of ministry in Indonesia would be, God had miraculously answered the prayers of so many people. Gordon was glad to be back at Jaffray College to dig himself out of a pile of unfinished business so abruptly abandoned in November 1986. His first priority was to complete his translations on his Daniel/Revelation class material.

While passing through Singapore on our way to Indonesia, Gordon purchased, with money that had been donated by friends in our Canadian churches, a word-processing Gestetner duplicator. It was to be given to the National Church when we retired. However, he soon realized that the Gestetner was too limiting for what he needed. He found a computer that met his needs and I used the Gestetner until we retired.

* * * * * * *

Dr. Peter Anggu reiterated the intrinsic purpose of a college library when he said: "The library's main function is to aid students to achieve their academic requirements. In fact, it should function as the heartbeat of the college." And he added, "In recent years students have come from numerous backgrounds to study at Jaffray College's undergraduate and graduate level programs. The ministry of the library is vital in motivating our students to be involved in the growth of Indonesian churches and the evangelization of unreached peoples." It could not have been said any better.

When Dr. Anggu asked me to help Mrs. Dee Bennett in the Jaffray College Library, I agreed but never dreamed what I would eventually be obligated to do. I'd had no library sciences training. To work in the library would be a learning exercise from the beginning. I familiarized myself with the one cataloging manual we had, checking the books that were on the library shelves with it.

Gordon had ordered the manual from the library at Union Theological Seminary in New York. It specifically outlined cataloguing procedures for theological colleges and was used by various institutions in the Far East and in Europe. Several years earlier, when a visiting library sciences specialist assisted at another theological college in Makassar, Dr. Anggu had asked Jerry Nanfelt to observe their upgrading process. She was then able to prepare a simple Indonesian manual for Jaffray College.

Since a generous gift came to purchase new books for the Jaffray College Library, there was an urgency to develop a more detailed library cataloging system for these materials. When Mrs. Bennett and her husband left for a year's home service assignment, I was assigned the job. That's when Gordon remembered that he had received resource materials from various theological schools. These colleges had shared information on upgrading our manual. Studying through those details, I discovered a program I could use.

I worked hard on upgrading the catalogue schedule into the Indonesian language, always conferring with our Jaffray College Indonesian staff on suitable subject headings. Gordon entered the headings into a computer file. During that process, he remembered a commitment he had made to the East Indonesia Kupang/Timor Indonesian workers when he had participated in their annual workers' retreat. They had requested a manual to catalogue the books they had in their theological school. Gordon's plan was for me to compile the relevant research, which he would computerize. Later he provided the resulting manual for his Kupang/Timor friends.

The Alliance College of Theology library in Australia was using the same database program. With the help of our missionary colleague, Bev Hendrickson in Australia, Gordon received templates to print necessary library cards for the Jaffray College Library in the Indonesian language. In the final edition of the Indonesian handbook, the groundwork was laid for the computerization of the cataloguing process as soon as Jaffray College could acquire the necessary staff. Though there was room for improvement in our cataloguing system, it was effectively used to meet our current needs.

Dr. Anggu kept urging us to prepare the library for the evaluation team from the Asian Theological Association, so that

Dr. Peter Anggu

Rev. Zefanya

Dr. Lawrence Kamasi

Rev. Titus Sampe

Dr. Yakob Tomatala

Dr. Magdalena G. Tomatala

Dr. Sadrak Kurang

Rev. B.R.S. Tinggi

Rev. Lolly Dungau

Rev. P.G.T. Sallipadang

Ivone Palar

Rev. Leo Sumule

Mr. Biring, M.A.

One of many families coming to
STTJ from Papua New Guinea
for graduate studies

Word of Life Publishers staff, c. 1972.
Rev. Udis, director; Rev. Bud Rudes, C&MA liason, centre front row

Jaffray College could become an accredited member. Gordon called the task "formidable". In January 1999, Jaffray College finally received word that they had received full accreditation—the only protestant theological college in Indonesia to receive the recognition at that time.

My work at the college, reclassifying 13,000 books, was more than formidable. Once again, God had a plan. Several of our brightest upperclassmen came to me saying, "I like what you are doing. May I help you?" What a miracle that was! Helping me after their class hours and on Saturdays, the College compensated them for their work.

More than ever, we needed a library sciences trained missionary. We had requested that the C&MA home office in the United States provide a librarian for a period of at least one term. They were never able to fill that request. The only help received was the assistance of Dr. Susan Schultz, a skilled librarian from Asbury Theological Seminary. She spent three weeks with us, checking our cataloging system and suggesting many improvements.

Jaffray College also hired a library sciences graduate from the main university in the city. He handled the loaning of books. I always tried to involve him in the library cataloguing changes that were being made. In my second year, several young men who had graduated from a library sciences course came to Jaffray College to do their internship. They reported that we had the most organized library in the city. That surprised me since Makassar had many colleges and universities.

I was delighted when two Jaffray College alumni came to me for a crash course in cataloging library books. They received their training in my office, and were able to take a photocopy of an Indonesian cataloguing handbook to their own theological schools.

* * * * * * *

As part of our ministry, we responded to people who came to our home requesting counseling. A Christian friend we met at our English Worship Fellowship had so much emotional conflict. "Things are all wrong," she said. As she shared her hurts, they didn't seem too problematic, but for release she needed to talk. Her husband enjoyed being involved with university students. Her two children in the senior high school level at Dalat School in

Penang enjoyed their peer relationships and their studies. In her mind they were so far away. After several comforting sessions and prayer she felt better. At the end of the school year the family returned to Australia.

This Australian friend then urged a native of Sri Lanka to get help from me also. Being a neighbour, she frequently visited. Her husband worked for The World Bank. Her two teenagers were quite involved in their studies in Singapore. She was distressed about family needs in Sri Lanka, but she also had deep personal needs. Though she was a Hindu, in one visit she asked for a Bible—saying she was open to learning about other religions. What I had was one extra English New Testament that came to me in bulk mailing from The Billy Graham Evangelistic Association. It just so happened that on the back of its title page it had a testimony of a Hindu convert to Christianity. In an added personal note he said that he hoped this book would bring as much peace to the reader as he had received. That shook her. When she came back to me she was infuriated because the New Testament talked about Jesus as the only way to heaven. She spoke her mind and returned home—to go into a Hindu fast. I continued visiting her. When they moved to Jakarta she phoned me and also wrote a letter to thank me for all my help. I'm not sure how I helped her. Heaven will tell the rest of the story.

Dr. Ilona came to me in mourning garb. She had been in Jakarta looking after a dying father, when back in our city, her doctor-husband had collapsed while jogging. She could not forgive herself for being absent when he died. Though she was a good Christian, she tried for weeks on her own to handle the acute pain of her grief. She couldn't even talk to her nine year-old daughter about it. Denial made recovery more difficult. The daughter finally broke the barrier when she talked about how she missed her father's love. That was the beginning of Ilona's release. In those days, I frequently visited her and prayed with her.

Nancy was a nominal Christian neighbor who had married a man from the majority religion. She was a young mother with two little girls and a two year-old boy whose sweet chatter cheered her every day. When her husband left her, he took the two girls with him. One day he asked to take the little boy for a walk. Nancy never saw them again. Although the courts decided that the father should have the two girls and that Nancy should have the boy, it never happened. When she heard that her son was living with an aunt in Jakarta, and that he had stopped talking and eating, she felt devastated. She told me of a potential study time in Jakarta to prepare her for a new job, which would also give her opportunity to visit her son. Neither the study time nor the chance to see her son materialized.

My heart ached for her when she came to me with her painful story. I told her about Jesus' love and prayed for her. The greatest encouragement she received was a simple booklet on how to become a follower of Christ. Not only did she cherish that study, she photocopied it and enthusiastically shared it with friends. When she returned home to visit her family, her father was pleased that she had come back into true faith. However, back in her city, being surrounded by neighbours who did not share her faith, she was harassed so much that she had to move and I lost track of her.

* * * * * * *

Many Jaffray College alumni pursued God's plan for their lives. Peter instructs, "Each one should use whatever gift he has received to serve others, faithfully administering God's grace in its various forms. If anyone speaks, he should do it as one speaking the very words of God. If anyone serves he should do it with the strength God provides, so that in all things God may be praised through Jesus Christ." (I Peter 4:10-11a) Our ministry priority in Makassar was training students at Jaffray College to follow in obedience to the Lord's call on their lives. In reality, our primary reward was watching God do extraordinary things through many ordinary alumni.

Sadrak Kurang and his wife Ribka had all the benefits of growing up in Christian homes in Toraja. After Sadrak graduated from Jaffray College he became our colleague on staff. He spoke of Gordon as a man who deeply influenced his own character. Sadrak and Gordon had frequent opportunities for friendly interaction on critical theological issues, social concerns and general knowledge. They were often found in animated dialogue, or even laughing and joking about trivial things—always building trust and respect for each other.

In 1987 Sadrak was invited to attend the Billy Graham "Barefoot Evangelism" seminar in Amsterdam, which increased his passion to reach more Indonesians with the good news of salvation in Jesus Christ. After that, he was appointed as Director of Evangelism at Jaffray College. At one point he took a five-member team to Papua where they served in sixteen churches. They held open-air meetings where four to five thousand people attended one meeting. They conducted Christian Education seminars, lay-training institutes and youth camps. It was no surprise that Sadrak involved Jaffray College students and staff to go out in evangelistic work at every opportunity, also ministering to unreached peoples.

When he was awarded a scholarship to take his doctoral studies at Fuller Theological Seminary in Pasadena, California, not only did he do well, his oldest son Teddy also finished his high school there with high marks. Teddy had a passion for Christian ministry and began studies at Asbury College, where he is currently studying for a Master's degree.

When Dr. Sadrak Kurang returned to Makassar in 1999 he was appointed Academic Dean of Jaffray College, which included multiple responsibilities. As a member of the college's Christian Education Committee, he spent days at a time evaluating and upgrading the teaching programs of all the National Church's schools of higher learning. In the 1999 college recess, he was also assigned to research the effectiveness of the National Church's functions, traveling to Jakarta and Yogyakarta in Java, and visiting many of the National Church's districts in Papua. In late 2001, Dr. Sadrak Kurang became President of Jaffray College.

Daniel Ronda's parents were members of a national C&MA church in Bali. Having attended Sunday school faithfully, it was an easy decision to become a Christian at 13 years of age. Subsequently, at a youth camp, when a Jaffray College student challenged the group to prepare to serve God, he raised his hand for prayer because he felt the Lord calling him to become a minister.

In 1985, as a freshman at Jaffray College, he said his instructors helped him both intellectually and spiritually. He appreciated Gordon for teaching him to think analytically, to read good books and to decide for himself why he should believe certain doctrines. He called Gordon one of his best mentors. What he valued most when visiting our home were Gordon's discussions on theology. In helping catalogue material for our college's library he learned to love good books, and said he learned to love God wholeheartedly because he saw Christ's love in me.

After Daniel graduated in 1990, together with his wife, Elisabet, they began a church-planting assignment in Ubud City,

Bali. Daniel was deeply burdened for the Balinese and praised God that he was able to lead many of them to Christ. He and his church members also built a place of worship.

In 1994 Dr. Anggu, President of Jaffray College, invited Daniel to return in order to teach freshmen and to earn a graduate degree at Jaffray College. By 1996 he was ready to study at The Alliance Bible Seminary in Manila, Philippines, where he earned a Master of Divinity degree. Later, also in Manila at The Asia Graduate School of Theology, he earned a Master of Theology degree and his wife earned a Partner in Ministry (PIM) degree.

When Daniel returned in 1999 to teach in the graduate program at Jaffray College, he shocked many people in his classes. If students were absent for part or all of a class they were asked to read 250 pages for every hour they were away, and were assigned to write an interactive paper. In no time students arrived on time and no one left early. Daniel became a highly respected teacher at the college. In 2003 he was thrilled to receive a scholarship toward doctoral studies at Asbury College in the USA. He would be taking six weeks of intensive training each semester, while still maintaining responsibilities at Jaffray College. That would certainly put him into a concentrated academic lifestyle. May God sustain him as he pursues these goals.

Mrs. Nel Tuhumury became a Christian when she was a university student in Makassar. She had been a nominal Christian, but while attending Inter-Varsity Fellowship meetings she began to understand the meaning of true Christianity. After she experienced her new life in Jesus Christ she became a passionate witness for her Lord. Later, when friends from Jaffray College realized her potential she came on staff as a teacher.

Nel was frequently asked to speak in churches, especially to address young people. She maintained her status as an ex-officio member of Inter-Varsity Fellowship in her city, and was involved in the National Prayer Movement in South Sulawesi. She also conducted a series of meetings in Sarawak, Malaysian Borneo, which created a rewarding opportunity for ministry.

Nel married Zeth Tuhumury, who worked in the administration office at Jaffray College. She praised God that we became her mentors to help them develop a stronger family relationship. When she was assigned to teach a new course called Christian Worship, she was thankful for Gordon's advice on how to manage it. Later, having an opportunity to take special courses in Singapore, she asked me to tutor her in intensive ESL classes so that she could better master those studies.

In October 1998, Mrs. Nel Tuhumury was the main speaker at the special Indonesia-wide GKII Ladies Retreat in Jakarta. Many of the delegates were Christian leaders, school teachers and political leaders. The most important event at the retreat for these leaders was to have time to share one-on-one with colleagues after the close of the evening service, discussing the demanding issues of their lives. Some wept and prayed till 4:00 a.m. and found glorious release and renewal. The Indonesian ladies were so grateful to Alliance Women in the USA who donated the money to finance the retreat.

Heber Agan and his wife, Yohana, had an intense burden to touch the lives of people who are very hard to reach. Heber became a Christian when he was in senior high school in Samarinda, East Borneo. Early in his Christian life, Jesus' words that permanently affected him were Acts 1:8, "But you will receive power when the Holy Spirit comes on you; and you will be my witnesses in Jerusalem, in all Judea and Samaria, and to the ends of the earth." He began to witness to people on the streets of his city and wherever he could reach them. He also prepared Bible studies for young people's groups.

When he came to study at Jaffray College he encountered severe physical problems. Because fevers persisted, a doctor was called in and diagnosed his illness as Leukemia with complications of hepatitis B—declaring it incurable. Though he had to quit his classes, his burden continued. He stayed on in Makassar taking private intensive ESL classes from me. After he returned to Samarinda God honored his faith and healed him.

Heber also became a world traveler visiting the Philippines, Singapore, Kuala Lumpur and Hong Kong. He traveled extensively in Australia, sharing the love of Jesus wherever he went.

Back in Samarinda, he began to witness to people in the city who didn't attend church. He fearlessly witnessed to people, sometimes receiving threatening phone calls because of it. By the year 2002 he was holding regular worship services in a downtown hotel where many business people and high school students attended. He provided special out-of-town meetings for 15 families who were reluctant to come to the hotel for fear of religious persecution. These were new believers living 35 kilometers from Samarinda. He also took frequent trips to

Balikpapan, a city 130 kilometers away, to conduct a worship service for a fair-sized international community. He praised God for opportunities to reach many people for Christ's Kingdom.

* * * * * * *

Papua New Guinea has a large community of GKII Christians. Some of them, like Yance Nawipa and Tibet Yikwa, took graduate studies at Jaffray College in our time and appreciated Gordon's photocopied lesson materials which they used in their home province. Some Papua alumni told about miraculous deliverances. Occult powers were prevalent even among some Christians. When C&MA retired missionaries visited the people they had served for years, they witnessed miraculous victories over occult powers, but not without intense prayer warfare by both them and their Indonesian brethren.

Some Jaffray College alumni, who were not born in Papua, were for years strong Christian leaders in that province. Rev. Pilemon Lappa, Director of STAKIN—a school teaching theology and community development—as well as Rev. Hendrik Yakob, Director of the Walter Post Theological College, and his wife, Kristiani, have contributed much to the Christian community in Papua for most of their lives. In 1999 these dear friends were not allowed to continue their work, probably because of an independence movement that was sweeping the province. Though the President of the country was able to stabilize the unrest, some problems remain. Rev. Benyamin Mangeka, also a teacher at STAKIN, was given an early pension, while his wife Maria continued as part-time teacher, office administrator, bookkeeper and treasurer.

* * * * * * *

Back in Makassar, during 1987, friends from evangelical churches in our city requested a seminar on Eschatology. In a large auditorium Gordon taught well over 500 people from 6:00 to 10:00 in the evening. For three nights he lectured on one of his favourite courses—Daniel/Revelation.

Meanwhile, Gordon's translations for his classes at Jaffray College consumed so much of his time that he began to call himself a "translat-aholic". On the one hand he was getting more skilled at translating quality materials, while on the other hand he felt driven to address current issues that kept surfacing in his classes. By carrying his lap-top computer to school, he used every spare minute. The appendix following this chapter shows the full extent of his translation work.

In our final days at Jaffray College, Gordon faced untreatable cancer. Many students as well as teachers, not only expressed their sympathies, but also their deep gratitude for the growth experience of being servants together in God's Kingdom. Coming from many of Indonesia's 27 provinces, as well as from Malaysian Borneo, it was a warm-hearted community of God's servants with a common vision. They appreciated valuable lessons learned in Gordon's classes. One said so descriptively, "When an elephant dies his ivory tusks remain!" Dr. Sadrak Kurang said he would always cherish the priceless fellowship times he'd had with Gordon. Dr. Anggu said that many students who didn't provide formal thanks were certainly included in the number of people who would never forget the experience of having Gordon as a teacher and mentor.

As President of Jaffray Theological College for most of our years at the college, Dr. Anggu left the most moving tribute of all for Gordon and me. He wrote:

> I claim myself as one of your co-workers who has benefited so much from your lives and your ministry. You were so wise in the stewardship of your money, your energies and your skills. You became the most productive missionaries since Dr. Jaffray's time, leaving many academic materials for our students and Christian leaders. I think especially of the late Gordon Chapman who seemed to sense the brevity of time, and maximized the use of the gifts God gave him. I long to follow in his footsteps.
>
> I envisioned that some day I could initiate a plan to name the Jaffray Theological College Library "The Adina Chapman Library", because she developed a more functional library cataloging system. [My reply to him was that such a prestigious title should really be given as "The Chapman Memorial Library" since Gordon was the library advisor for years and since he collected the materials which I used. I merely did the research and recatalogued the books, while he computerized the program. –a.c.]
>
> When the issue arose that you shouldn't return to Jaffray Theological College because you didn't have degrees, my answer was, "An academic degree does not guarantee teaching

ability." [Then he mentioned the names of many Jaffray Theological College alumni that we had taught who were currently top leaders in ministry. –a.c.]

Mr. Chapman was my highly valued advisor. When I had written my letter of resignation, he begged me with tears not to resign but to remain strong. I would certainly have handed in my letter of resignation except for his reassuring words. To this day I'm thankful for his encouragement.

In a few months I will reach retirement age by our National Church standards, except that my tenure of service doesn't end until two years from now. I praise God that by His grace, it could be said that I have completed my service well, even though I often made mistakes. I am rightfully proud that numerous alumni and friends have been prepared to take up the burdens of Christian ministry after us. Many of them will serve their Lord even better than we did.

With deepest respect, peace to you,
Peter Anggu

When Gordon passed away, his missionary colleagues wrote the following tribute:

Rev. Gordon Chapman—retired Alliance missionary, died October 27, 1993, in Calgary, Alberta. He was 67 years old. To those of us who served with him in Indonesia he was a very unique, gifted, humorous man—a co-worker who will always be remembered with great respect for his quick wit and winning smile. Gordon was best known as a teacher and translator. In early 1991, even though he knew he had untreatable cancer, he returned to finish his work before officially retiring in 1992.

Perhaps most telling are Dr. Anggu's capsulated words, "Mr. Chapman was very well known and loved by churches all over South Sulawesi as one whose preaching was characterized by sharp, critical exposition of Scripture to build up the body of Christ."

With a laugh, Mr. Chapman would marvel that he, with only a Bachelors' degree, would be teaching on a seminary level. The fact of the matter was, Rev. Chapman had been a constant reader and was a self-educated man. He taught with depth and quality that his students say will be difficult to forget.

The residents of heaven have welcomed him as one who has faithfully run the race, all the way to the finish line. But we'll miss him very much.

See you in heaven, Gordon,
Your Indonesian family

* * * * * * *

In all our ventures in Indonesia we could not achieve our goals by labouring alone. By working hand in hand with Indonesian and missionary colleagues, by working alongside all our alumni throughout the country, God had indeed helped us to *embrace the mountain* for His Kingdom. That was the winning factor.

Gordon V. Chapman, 1926 - 1993

APPENDIX I

List of works translated by Rev. Gordon V. Chapman

The following is a summary, prepared from Gordon Chapman's records, of all the teaching materials he prepared in the Indonesian language. In some cases Gordon added translations to supplement what others had produced. These were originally used at Jaffray Theological College. At the end of this report are listed the bibliographies of these translations and the names of the qualified Indonesian language speakers on whom he always relied to check his translations in detail. Above all, Gordon's primary goal was to never violate the original author's copyright, nor infringe upon the precise interpretation of his thoughts. Titles in both the Indonesian and English languages are for the reader's benefit.

What Paul said in II Timothy 4:13 is so significant, "When you come, bring the cloak that I left with Carpus at Troas, and my scrolls, especially the parchments." Paul needed his cloak in the cold prison cell, but most of all he needed the comfort of "the parchments". Gordon guarded his manuscripts most carefully. These titles mirror the chapters of his life:

Ajaran Daniel/The Message of Daniel by Arthur Petrie, Th. D. [Christian Publications]

Eskatologi/Eschatology—consisted of selected excerpts from the following authors: Gleason L. Archer, Robert G. Clouse, William W. Conley and selected excerpts from *The Book of Books: Major Prophet* by Murray Downey [Christian Publications]; *The Book of Books: The Gospel of John and Revelation* by Murray Downey [self published]; *The Church and the Tribulation* by Robert Gundry [Gordon had no information on the publisher]; *The End Times* by Herman A. Hoyt [Moody Press]; *The Truth About Armageddon* by William Sanford LaSor [Baker]; *The Approaching Advent of Christ* by Alexander Reese [Marshall, Morgan and Scott]; *Tribulation Or Rapture—Which?* by Oswald

J. Smith [Sovereign Grace Advent Testimony]; and four articles from *Christian Life*, May 1974.

Etika Kristen/Christian Ethics, a compilation of class notes, by David H. Moore and his assistant Robert Lessnusa, edited and updated in 1988 by Gordon Chapman with supplemental excerpts from: *The Right To Live, The Right To Die* by Everett C. Koop [Gordon had no information on the publisher], former Surgeon General of the U.S.A. Other topics include, divorce and remarriage, and abortion, with excerpts from: *Baker's Dictionary of Theology* and *Baker's Dictionary of Christian Ethics* [Baker]; Minutes of the C.& M.A. Annual Council, 1976, (pp. 262-267), and finally, a statement drawn up by the faculty of Jaffray Theological College on Divorce and Remarriage, in August, 1979.

Kitab Di Atas Segala Kitab/The Book Of Books, vol.4: *Major Prophets* by Murray Downey [Christian Publications]

Kitab Di Atas Segala Kitab/The Book Of Books, vol.9: *Letters To Jewish Believers* by Murray Downey [self published]

Kitab Wahyu/The Revelation by James McConkey [The Silver Publishing Co.] (James McConkey was best known for: *The Threefold Secret of The Holy Spirit* [recently published by Back to the Bible Broadcast, Lincoln, Nebraska, U.S.A.]—a book they distributed at no charge to interested people.)

Melampaui Kepribadian, Konsepsi Kristiani Tentang Allah/Beyond Personality, The Christian Concept of God by Geoffrey Bles, which is now Book Four in *Mere Christianity* by C. S. Lewis [Macmillan]

Menuju Kepada Pengertian Tentang Surat Roma/Towards Understanding Romans, Part I by Boyce Blackwelder [Warner Press, Anderson, Indiana] (Only the first half of the book is included in this translation. The second half—not translated—was *An Exegetical Translation of the Book of Romans*.)

Pengantar Kitab Daniel/Introduction to Daniel by Joyce G. Baldwin, Charles F. Pfeiffer, a compilation of excerpts from *Daniel: an Introduction and Commentary* by Joyce G. Baldwin [IVP]; Excerpts from the *NIV Study Bible* [Zondervan]; and

Daniel and Minor Prophets with excerpts from *Wycliffe Bible Commentary*, editor Charles F. Pfeiffer [Iverson]

Sedjarah Pengutusan Indjil/History of Missions by Dr. Robert Glover, et al. (This book was first translated and compiled by Miss Lela Pierce in the 1960s in West Borneo, based on *The Progress of World Missions* by Dr. Robert Glover [Gordon had no information on the publisher], and *The Missionary Atlas: a manual of the foreign work of the Christian and Missionary Alliance* [Christian Publications]. It was checked by M. Silalahi and printed in Makassar in 1970.)

Serba-Serbi Tentang Kerajaan Allah/Miscellaneous Truths on The Kingdom of God, excerpts from: *The Gospel of The Kingdom: Scriptural Studies in the Kingdom of God*, chapter 2, *The Kingdom Tomorrow* by George E. Ladd [Wm. Eerdmans]; and *UNTIL: The Coming of Messiah and His Kingdom*, with *Appendix A: Was Pentecost The Coming of the Kingdom? Appendix B: The Rhetorical Mode of the Prophets. Appendix C: The Time Frame of the Olivet Prophecy. Appendix F: The Church and Premillennialism* by Robert Shank [Westcott]

Serba-Serbi Tentang Kitab Wahyu/Miscellaneous Truths on Revelation with excerpts from the following works: *A Commentary on The Revelation of John, Introduction* by George E. Ladd [Wm. Eerdmans]; *The Book of Books*, vol.10: *The Gospel of John* and *The Book of Revelation, Revelation Surveyed* by Murray W. Downey [self-published]; and *UNTIL: The Coming of Messiah and His Kingdom*, with additional excerpts from *Appendix D: The Chronological Structure of Revelation, and Appendix E: Revelation Twenty* by Robert Shank [Westcott]

Tantangan & Respons : Suatu Pedoman Tentang Apologetika Kristen/Challenge and Response : A Guide to Christian Apologetics by Fredric R. Howe [Gordon had no information on the publisher]

Terpilih Dalam Anak: Suatu Penyelidikan Tentang Doktrin Pilihan/Elect in The Son: A Study of the Doctrine of Election by Robert Shank [Westcott] (This book is incomplete in that only chapter 4 and two appendices of *Elect in the Son* were translated and checked. Gordon had completed chapters 2 & 3 in rough form only.)

Teologia Alkitab; Angelologi & Antropologi/Biblical Theology; Angelology and Anthropology This book and the following books are translations of Stanton W. Richardson's three-volume *Biblical Theology series*. They were published in mimeographed form with spiral binding, by St. Paul Bible College. (To Gordon's translation of *Angelology and Anthropology* was added a three page supplement, written by David Moore. In the section on Anthropology, Gordon added supplemental excerpts on abortion, including some full-colour brochures.)

Teologia Alkitabiah; Bibliologi & Teologi/Bibliology and Theology Proper prepared by Richard K. Smith. (Gordon added excerpts from *The Remarkable Birth of Planet Earth* by Henry Morris [Gordon had no information on the publisher], and two sections and appendices from *Scientific Creationism*, written by the technical staff and consultants of the Institute of Creation Research [Creation Life Publishers]

Teologia Alkitabiah: Ekklisiologi/Biblical Theology: Ecclesiology. (Gordon's translations in this book are in the first section: from Stanton Richardson's series, and two chapters added from *Servants in Charge* by Keith Bailey [Christian Publications]. The second section contains Dick Smith's notes on Ecclesiology, supplemented by Gordon Chapman's excerpts from *Acts One and Two : assessing the interpretation of receiving the Holy Spirit and the related spiritual gifts in the initial formation of the Church*.)

Teologia Alkitabiah: Kristologi & Soteriologi/Biblical Theology: Christology and Soteriology translated by Gordon Chapman. (This book is in two parts: translations from *Stanton Richardson's book*, and five appendices from *Life in the Son* by Robert Shank [Westcott], and Lecture XXXVI from *Lectures on Theology* by Charles Finney [Colporter Kemp].)

Teologia Alkitabiah: Pneumatologi/Biblical Theology: Pneumatology by Stanton W. Richardson. (The text is about one third of Stanton Richardson's *Lectures on Pneumatology*. Gordon regretted that, for lack of time, he was not able to finish translating this excellent material. Dr. Richardson was head of the Department of Theology at St. Paul Bible College in Minnesota.)

In summary, Stanton W. Richardson's materials Gordon translated as listed above were: *Bibliology, Angelology, Anthropology, Christology, Soteriology, Ecclesiology, Eschatology and Pneumatology*.

Angaran Dasar Gereja Kemah Injil Indonesia/The Statement of Faith of The Gospel Tabernacle of Indonesia Dr. Anggu especially expressed appreciation for Gordon Chapman's translation and promotion of this invaluable permanent record for the Indonesian National Church.

* * * * * * *

Indonesian language speakers on whom Gordon depended to check his translations were: Mr. Biring, Rev. John Sandi Dana, Rev. Sadrak Kurang, and Rev. M. Silalahi.

As a teacher, Gordon was dearly loved by his students for his interesting lectures, and for the freedom he encouraged in class discussions. His translations are highly valued by numerous evangelical leaders in many denominations in Indonesia. Since the year 2000, because an Indonesian Christian leader requested Gordon's translations, they are being sent out by electronic mail—under the direction of Rev. Daniel Ronda at Jaffray Theological College. The College has copies of all the original translations. In this way Gordon's Indonesian translations are being received by an ever-growing audience.

Gordon was an excellent extemporaneous translator, often being called upon to translate for foreign guest speakers. He was asked to be the translator for Dr. Don Richardson's seminar lectures at Jaffray Theological College on *Eternity In Their Hearts*. Don Richardson, who was also the author of *Peace Child* and *Lords of the Earth,* requested of Gordon, "Next time I come to Indonesia, please travel with me as my translator." Dr. Richardson remembered enough of the Indonesian language from his Papua missionary days to understand how well his lectures were being relayed. Unfortunately, he did not return during our time.

APPENDIX II

English translation of :
Salam Bahagia di Dalam Kristus Yesus

Greetings in the Name of Jesus Christ

Grace and peace from God our Father and the Lord Jesus Christ be with you all. In the love of Christ I send greetings to you, our fellow colleagues and alumni in Indonesia, with the apostle Paul's words in II Corinthians 3:2-3, "You yourselves are our letter, written on our hearts, known and read by everybody. You show that you are a letter from Christ, the result of our ministry, written not with ink but with the Spirit of the living God, not on tablets of stone but on tablets of human hearts."

Just as the apostle Paul praised God for the faithfulness of God's children in Corinth, so I also praise the Lord that you have become Christ's letter that can be read by all men for the glory of God in your places of service. Furthermore, I praise God that He gave us the opportunity to serve you in a precious fellowship that comforts me to this day. May the love of Jesus Christ and the power of God's Spirit continue to equip you for service for the glory of the Lord.

Forgive me if the events written in this publication do not tell all the things each of you have experienced. What has been written are merely examples of how, with the help of the Lord, you have had victories in each of your areas. I trust that whatever has been reported will present a balance between the difficulties you encountered and the victories you have won.

In all these things I praise the Lord, that together with you, He gave us the opportunity to *embrace the mountain*, for the far-reaching extension of the Kingdom of God for His Glory. " ... being confident of this, that he who began a good work in you will carry it on to completion until the day of Christ Jesus." (Philippians 1:6)

The grace of our Lord Jesus be with you,
Mrs. Adina Chapman
—November 2003